French Twist

A Refreshingly Frank Travel Memoir by a Modern American Puritan

Elizabeth Bingham
Author of *French Survival Guide*
and *German Shepherd*

World Prospect Press
Waverly, Iowa

World Prospect Press
P.O. Box 253
Waverly, IA 50677
www.worldprospect.com

Publisher's Cataloging-in-Publication
(Provided by Quality Books, Inc.)

Bingham, Elizabeth.
   French twist : a refreshingly frank travel memoir by a modern American Puritan / Elizabeth Bingham. -- First edition.
   pages cm
   Includes index.
   LCCN 2015938682
   ISBN-13: 978-0-9703734-1-0
   ISBN-10: 0-9703734-1-4

   1. Bingham, Elizabeth--Travel--France. 2. France--Description and travel. 3. France-Social life and customs. 4. Travel writers--United States--Biography. 5. Travelers' writings, American. I. Title.

DC29.3.B526 2015   914.404'84
                              QBI15-600091

Printed in the United States of America

Table of Contents

From the Author

This travel memoir has been a joy to work on. To mentally relive my trips to France with my good friend and various family members, to re-experience the highs and the lows, the confusions and the delights—what fun! After years of writing educational language and culture guides for tourists, it was a welcome change of pace to switch to a lighter subject, a more informal style. Now I could confess in addition to advise, reveal the mistakes that led to the insights. As a fully fallible human, I had plenty of errors and miscues to share!

I hope this book serves as a companion to *French Survival Guide*, that it is an easy way to learn more about French culture and what to expect as a visitor in France. It offers a behind-the-scenes peek at the process that goes into researching and testing the material of my language and culture guides. I freely confess (as I have elsewhere) that I am not fluent in French. But I do know how to learn and teach foreign languages (Ph.D. from the University of Texas at Austin), and I use myself as a guinea pig to experience France as a novice and share what I've learned to help others. (Don't worry—I also work with French experts to make sure I get it right.)

In that spirit, I hope this book helps prepare readers to travel in France and to attempt the language. If it inspires them to make the leap in the first place and actually visit the country, so much the better. Or if it serves instead as substitute travel for those who are not able to take a trip themselves, well, that is also a worthy goal and I embrace it happily.

I tried to be as honest and accurate as I could in writing this book. That reasonable guideline turned out to be a major pain in the neck, leading to endless corrections and rewrites throughout the process (in addition to many unflattering self-portrayals). Still, I no doubt erred in some of my memories, depictions, and explanations, and for that I apologize.

I feel I need to explain the "modern American Puritan" portion of this book's subtitle, as a couple of family members have raised questions about it, thinking it doesn't apply to me, a generally liberal thinker. That's why I put "modern" in there. I'm not completely old-fashioned, after all. The "American" part is to emphasize that this book about France is from an American perspective. As for the "Puritan" label that some people object to, well, I think it applies. I know I am comparatively prudish and moralistic—a Puritan in the modern American sense. At least, that's what makes sense to me.

While I'm at it, I'll address the first part of the subtitle, as well: "A Refreshingly Frank Travel Memoir." The "frank" part is because I include details and observations that I'm not necessarily comfortable sharing with the world, but which I think are interesting in themselves or add interest to our story by revealing more of the situations Micki and I found ourselves in. I'm not normally fixated on bathroom matters, for example, but when you're a traveler, then those things take on added importance. I also like the word "frank" because that is the name of the Germanic tribe that populated northern France and gave the country its name. As for "refreshingly," that word was suggested by an early reader and supported by others. Personally, I thought "shockingly explicit" would grab readers' attention much better, but I couldn't justify that as even remotely accurate.

I would like to briefly acknowledge the people who most contributed to this book, although their contributions and my gratitude would justify a full chapter, at least.

First and foremost, I take my hat off to Micki Reints, my cheerful travel companion, who endured the worst of our days with the best of humor. She is open to adventure and generous with her time and encouragement, and I have her full permission to share the details of our escapades. Our visit to France was the first of several trips we have now taken together, and I hope to have a whole "Travels with Micki" series to share with the world before we hang up our passports for quieter pursuits. Thanks go to Micki's husband, Jeff, as well, for his good-natured acceptance of losing his wife for two weeks so we could venture to France together.

While Micki is present throughout these pages, I also benefitted greatly from other travel companions who make smaller appearances in this book: Beverly Moffitt, Elaina Toenjes, Bruce Toenjes, John Toenjes, Rachel Toenjes Zander, and Emily Bingham. Thanks also to David Zelle for sharing his French travel experiences. These people all enriched my travels and enlivened the stories I have to tell about our visits.

My excellent editors deserve thanks and praise beyond what I can include here. Linda Bingham and David Zelle provided invaluable comments and corrections on a late version of this manuscript. If any clunky prose or inaccurate details remain, it is completely my own responsibility (probably for unwisely ignoring their advice on occasion). Other readers whose input shaped this work include John Zelle, Emily Bingham, and Treasa Lindaman. Thank you for your suggestions, questions, and encouragement!

As always, I am deeply grateful to my husband for his unending support and technical assistance. My travels, writing, and publishing would not be possible without him, to say nothing of our two delightful children. Yes, *both* of them.

Part I: Paris

1
The Raven and the Butterfly

The first time I went to France, I came back pregnant.

I wrote the words in a pre-trip email to amuse my friend and travel companion, Micki. Or, more accurately, I wrote them to torment Micki's husband, Jeff, who was convinced his petite blond wife was going to be the object of endless male admiration when we traveled to France in a few weeks.

True! And our hotel owner's name was Paul! Coincidence. I swear it.

Paul was also the name that my husband John and I gave the baby who appeared a little more than eight months after that first Paris trip, and who was now my 7 ½-year-old. John had not accompanied me on that trip to France, and it had been a running joke between us ever since that Paul was my little French boy.

The whole French trip with Micki came about as a fluke, because of cheap airfare to Rome. Or, rather, before that, it came about because my dear German "mother" generally calls my household to greet us on birthdays and major holidays. Technically, Inge is a distant relative on my husband's side, but she has housed me numerous times in her beautiful home, and I'm very close to her. Every time I get off the phone after those calls, I long to see her again and thus start checking out flights to Berlin. They're always pricey, so I start looking at other destinations for better deals because I am a complete travel junky and can't help myself. This happened again in early June, on my daughter Emily's 12th birthday. Right on schedule, the phone rang. I chatted with Inge. I smiled hugely and laughed and desperately dredged up my half-buried German vocabulary. Then, sadly, I hung up.

And I hit Expedia.

Berlin, as usual, was too expensive to consider for an impromptu trip, but before long I stumbled on a fantastic roundtrip price from Cedar Rapids, Iowa (my usual airport), to Rome in September, only $550. *$550!* That's all it takes to set me off on a multi-day travel obsession. The Eternal City at the start of the shoulder season. Gauzy visions of the Roman Forum, of the Spanish Steps, of St. Peter's Basilica rose before my eyes—*Roman Holiday* minus only Gregory Peck and Audrey Hepburn.

I actually mapped out a quick two-week visit for my daughter and me before reality set in—it wasn't fair to dump our son's school schedule on my husband in September, when his own college-teaching duties also shifted into high gear. Not just so I could gallivant across Italy, anyway. So I did the responsible thing and reluctantly gave up dreams of Rome and Venice for Emily and me. But such a lost opportunity, tickets to Italy and back for only $550! It was unheard of.

I was grumbling about missing that unbelievable deal when I was at our church shortly thereafter, which is how Micki entered the picture.

Micki had been involved in the Sunday School program at our church since she was a young bride, more than 25 years before, long before I came to settle there. I had been on board only five or six years, but had been active in that time and had come to know Micki pretty well and value her highly. In mid-June, as in every June, we were up to our necks in our Vacation Bible School program, our annual summer self-punishment to aid the moral and Christian development of our local children.

Our morning Bible School program concluded with sack lunch mayhem before families came to reclaim their children. At that point, we teachers could sigh in the relief of one more day behind us and then set about cleaning up the spilled lemonade, chips, and cookie bits the kids left behind in sticky profusion. Between wiping tables and sweeping the floor one day, I told Micki about my disappointment in not being able to jump on the terrific airfare to Rome. She looked wistful and shared that she had never been to Europe, but would like to go some day. Her husband, a gentle bear of a man, would never go because he couldn't tolerate long flights on a cramped plane.

My brain lit up. I went home from church and did a little research online that afternoon. After a short consultation, Micki and I decided to visit France.

Our combined schedules allowed only a brief open window in August, which determined *when* we would travel—the height of the tourist season. As for *where*, while Micki was game to travel anywhere, we settled on France for a practical reason: it was the most useful business expense for me at that time.

I write and publish European language and culture books for American tourists (very slowly, I should note), and my current project was a guide for travelers to France. While I had been to France before, my previous excursions had been confined to Paris and its environs. A longer trip with

Micki would afford the chance to venture beyond the heart of France and, for the first time, the opportunity to drive a car instead of taking public transportation everywhere. The trip promised multiple rewards: fun travel with a friend, the chance to work on my tourist French, and new experiences to share with future readers.

I'm like a drug addict with trip planning, glued to my computer or travel books for days on end—a real binge— and neglecting my duties as mom and household manager. We had cereal for supper, the mail stacked up, and clean laundry was a distant memory, but soon I had laid out a sweet trip: five days in Paris, two in Normandy, three in châteaux country. (Singular: château. Plural: châteaux. Welcome to French.) Everything fell into place.

Hi, Micki. Almost all our hotels are booked. (We get to stay on the island of Mont Saint-Michel!!!) It worked better to tour counterclockwise, so here's the updated itinerary. Paris agendas are very flexible. We may want to move things around, depending on the weather. If you want to make sure to include something that isn't already there, let me know.

I kept asking Micki for her preferences, but she kept replying, "Whatever you want to do is fine," which makes her sound like a pushover, and she's anything but. She can organize an event and marshal her troops and take charge in the kitchen like the most efficient general, while I stand around slack-jawed, unsure what to do, where to start. On a trip abroad, however, our roles were reversed, and she deferred to my experience.

By the end of June, with our itinerary, lodging, and transportation lined up, I began to think about trip clothes. This is a bit like a vegan planning the Thanksgiving feast, because I am the most boring dresser this side of the Amish, but I wanted to 1) maximize combinations so I could take as little as possible, 2) keep to darks and neutrals that wouldn't show every speck of dirt, and 3) choose items whose nationality was vague so I wouldn't be immediately identifiable as an American from two blocks away.

Now, before all the "America-first" supporters start accusing me of being anti-American and pelting me with their U.S. flags (probably made in China), I would like to explain that I've been to Europe many times, and I've lived there for a couple of stretches. I have many dear friends there. So, yes, to a certain extent I identify with Europeans.

Just as important, though, I prefer not to stand out any time, but especially not when I travel, and I can tell you from my occasional quasi-European perspective that many American tourists do, indeed, stand out negatively. Dress and actions that are perfectly normal and acceptable at home are not necessarily attractive abroad. Different societies have different social practices, and adapting to those does not mean someone hates their home country. What this meant for my August travel wardrobe was neutral colors, skirts and capris, no tennis shoes, and no shorts. I would be a symphony of brown, black, and tan.

I'll try to downsize my packing. I've been known to go overboard.
Micki

Micki is the anti-Amish in her dress. Not that she's a Vegas showgirl, but she does love her bling and her bright colors. Hot pinks and greens, warm corals and pastels—she loves them all, and they suit her blue-eyed blond looks and upbeat personality. She color-coordinates her jewelry, with a particular fondness for sparkle and shine.

Micki was going to tone down her normal color exuberance for our trip—also not wanting to stand out—but next to her I would look like a funeral director (which I can claim with some authority, because I once worked in a funeral home).

I'm not even going to try the language. I'm leaving that all up to you! Micki

My next item of business was to work on French so I would be able to communicate at a basic tourist level, as necessary. I know from painful experience that complete ignorance of the local language gets in the way of the best experience possible. Imagine monolingual French tourists coming to the United States and trying to communicate using just their native tongue. *Pouvez-vous m'aider s'il vous plaît?* They wouldn't get very far. While their French accents may be charming, their lack of English would spur bafflement, frustration, and resentment among many in the U.S. In France, I wanted to do better than that and at least be able to ask, "Which wine do you recommend?" and "Where are the toilets?" before having to resort to pantomime. The French are famously reserved. I can't imagine they would react well to any charade demonstrating the need for a toilet.

You can assure Jeff that I travel like a nun.

Jeff continued to worry about Micki, his bright butterfly, attracting men in France. There was no real concern on his part, we all knew, just a gentle teasing from a devoted husband who was facing the longest separation from his high-school-sweetheart wife that he'd ever had to endure. But Micki was safe with me, the undertaker. I really did travel like a nun (at least, how I imagined a nun would travel), in my modest, sober clothes and sensible shoes, earnestly viewing the sights, avoiding all nightlife, all flirtatious situations. I was as reliable a travel companion as a Labrador retriever.

Our trip preparations continued. I picked up my vital

prescription patches from the pharmacy, grateful that they would spare me the motion sickness I had suffered on my first trans-Atlantic flight, many years before. I had ordered a debit card for my business checking account, to back up my regular ATM card. The prevalence of cash machines abroad made getting local currency much easier and more convenient than in the days of traveler's checks and money exchanges, but they carried a certain risk: the cash cards sometimes malfunctioned in the ATMs, leaving hapless tourists without money to spend. I would travel with my ATM card *and* my debit card *and* a credit card, and with Micki bringing along multiple options, as well, we should be safe on the money front.

We planned our adventure on such short notice that I didn't even have a valid passport. (Raising young children for the previous decade, I had severely cut back on international travel.) I quickly reapplied for one, paid for expedited service, and prayed that the rumored multi-month backlog was not going to torpedo my trip. The expedited processing came through as promised, however, and on July 14 (Bastille Day! What an omen!), I found my new passport in the mail. I checked out the picture. It wasn't too bad—I had long brown hair, a typical black shirt, and I was smiling broadly, happily anticipating my travels.

Micki, on the other hand, wasn't so pleased with hers.

"I look like a prison guard," she grumbled.

I allowed that it was a very sober look for her.

"They told me not to smile!" she wailed.

We shared photocopies of our passports with each other as back-ups in case we lost our originals on our trip. It was a novel experience that I looked brighter than Micki, my smiling visage next to her stern stare. I promised I wouldn't show hers to anyone.

In mid-July, I met Micki during coffee after church. We had a preliminary discussion of what to pack.

"How many pairs of shoes should I take?"

"Two," I advised. "Both comfortable. So you have a dry pair in case one gets rained on."

Raincoat? (Yes.) Shorts? (Long ones are OK.) I found out that Micki can't drive a stick shift, so there would be no point in putting two drivers on the car reservation. Neither of us had ever used GPS before (an option with the car rental), so I decided we would be OK relying on maps. (Micki was less confident than I was, I recalled later, but at the time I was sure we would be fine.) We briefly discussed money belts versus passport pouches. However, with disturbing images seared into my memory of travel-show host Rick Steves demonstrating how to access *his* money belt—pulling up his shirt like a doughy white striptease—I quickly axed the money belt idea. I was pretty sure that my mushy maternal midsection would make Rick look like Adonis. Micki and I would take our chances with passport pouches. We could wear them securely under our shirts, just around our necks, rather than on our waists.

Amid all my trip preparations, our regular life had not been put on hold. Son Paul had his guitar lessons. John and daughter Emily had drum lessons. During one of these lesson periods at our local music store, I left the others and dashed to the nearby stores to load up on possible clothes and shoes to take home for try-on. I was acutely aware that I would be traveling with fashion-conscious Micki, and my own travel wardrobe was desperate for a facelift. So one week during music lessons, I gathered the possibilities, and the next week, I returned the rejects. I ended up keeping a pair of outrageously expensive hiking sandals for their sturdiness and comfort, along with capris, shirts, and a skirt. I also bought a couple of black tote bags in my ongoing search for the perfect travel bag.

Micki and I met later that day—not to discuss the itinerary or French history or the art masterpieces we would see—but to consider luggage. We discussed carry-ons, my black options and her terracotta-colored one. We would both take a backpack and a tote bag on the plane, with the tote counting as a (yes, very large) purse, and we would check small suitcases, wheeled and expandable, in case we would go crazy buying souvenirs.

I showed her the new hiking sandals I had on, raving about how comfortable they were.

"Say," it occurred to me, "don't you have some like these?"

Not only like them, but *identical* to them, just a size smaller. We had bought them from different stores, in different towns, at the recommendation of different clerks, but they were the same shoes. We both liked them too much for either of us to give them up, though, and decided we didn't care if we had matching footwear.

I left all my France books and maps with Micki, hoping she would pore over them and get a feel for Paris and the métro system, and also to get them out of *my* hands. The rest of my life, the previously scheduled, non-France part of my life, continued its roll, and I had a family Minnesota lake vacation to prepare for. I didn't leave France entirely behind, though. In Minnesota, I sat on our deck alongside Lake Superior and worked my way through a draft copy of my next book, *French Survival Guide*. I edited and, in the process, reviewed the language material we would have to rely on once Micki and I left the safe, English-speaking cocoon of Tourist Central around Paris.

My previous French trips had shown me that any ability in that language would be useful. Not everyone speaks English, and even many of those who *do* avoid using it, often out of the fear of revealing imperfections. Language standards are so high regarding their native tongue that venturing into a non-native language can be paralyzingly intimidating for

French people. As an American, however, I had very few of those qualms. I came from a land of sloppy speakers and writers, where entire conversations can be constructed out of vague expressions punctuated by endless *dude*s or, like, *stuff*, and no one cares about distinctions between *to, two,* and *too* or *there, their,* and *they're* anymore. By God, I'm not afraid to make mistakes in a foreign language. And I frequently do.

My lack of French inhibitions and my general willingness to make a fool of myself in that language stretch back to that original trip to Paris, the one I came back from to discover I was pregnant. On a drizzly March day, my grandmother and I popped into a McDonald's on the Champs-Élysées for hot tea and a snack. I ordered in careful, labored French. The young worker smiled at me, amused by my bad accent, but took the order. I smiled back, acknowledging my linguistic clumsiness, but secretly flush with victory. I had communicated in French, and I had broken through the fabled French reserve and briefly connected with a local. Granted, it was probably an immigrant worker who doubtless lacked the true French dignity and French disdain for language errors, but I would savor any linguistic connection I could. Preparing for the Micki trip, my brief French review in Minnesota was not enough to give me any real fluency in the language, but at least we had a linguistic safety net for the most basic communications.

Aug. 4—Hi, Micki,

*We're back from Minnesota and had a great time. Now, looking ahead. Are we seriously leaving for France in FOUR DAYS??????
Whose CRAZY IDEA was this?????? Argh!!!! Time to start laundry and buy school supplies. And work on plumbing. (Did I mention that the morning we left, a cracked bathroom fixture started to leak through the living room ceiling?) And work with KCRG TV to try to set up a commercial shoot and a blues-guitarist job shadow for Paul. (We got*

word on vacation that Paul had won a writing contest they sponsored.)
OF COURSE this all had to happen while I'm gone. Do you mind
traveling in France with a bald lady? I AM bringing a hat, after all.

That two-week open stretch in August that we had aimed
our trip for in June had ballooned into a bloated schedule of
important appointments by the time we reached it. While Micki
and I would be in France, I would miss my young son's first
TV commercial shoot, his first CT scan, and his first allergy
test, all events that had not even been on the horizon earlier
in the summer. But the trip was set, and go we must, even if
I was figuratively pulling all my hair out.

Micki and I continued to wrestle the weighty question of
what bags we should take to best meet our needs. I returned
the two black tote bags I'd tried out from Kohl's; they were
no better than black bags that I already had. I decided to go
with an enormous business tote bag I'd previously ordered
to haul my wide laptop and projects in so I could take my
work on vacation with me. (As a writer who sets my own
hours—both at home and on vacation—I was not afraid of
overworking myself.)

With this huge boxy bag slung over my shoulder in France,
I would be in constant danger of sideswiping and jabbing un-
suspecting bystanders on the métro and in other crowds, but
it was relatively light, and it more than accommodated my
needs and wants for a day of touring—guidebooks, language
books, water bottle, snacks, umbrella, sweater, camera, the odd
loaf of bread and bottle of wine. In addition, my document
bag, with passport and money, usually ended up in there as
well, because it felt more secure (although it probably wasn't)
clamped under my arm than it did hanging diagonally across
my body. (I had quickly abandoned the idea of the vinyl passport pouch under my shirt in sweltering August. It was simply
too uncomfortable and inconvenient to pull it out every time

I needed to access my passport. And, frankly, my chest wasn't flat enough to carry it off without odd bumps jutting out.)

Micki solved her security concerns by buying a cross-body document bag with a steel cable running through the strap. Her "vault" (as the company referred to it) also had locking zipper clasps and wire mesh in the lining to thwart slash-and-grab thefts. I had lusted after these bags in travel magazines and catalogs for years, but had never thought the additional safety features justified the extra expense.

I questioned that assumption on this trip, though. We imagined ourselves vulnerable to stealthy pickpockets on every métro train, at every crowded tourist sight, on every busy street—pretty much everywhere I would be banging into people with my big tote bag, in other words. But Micki's high-security vault and my iron arm clamp would see us safely through those dangers.

Comparing our bags was the reason I stopped at her house just two days before our departure. She had luggage strewn around the dining room, and her dining room table was piled with stacks of clothes, including a tower of colorful underwear.

"I see you have your thongs ready to go," I deadpanned. Someone had joked about how we would need to pack thongs for our visit to sinful old Paris, home of depraved hedonism.

Micki snorted and rolled her eyes. "Right! Me, in a thong! Good old cotton underwear."

In the case of a horrible accident in France, the Lutheran Sunday School Brigade was not going to shock anyone at home with our underwear choices. The dancers on Montmartre might kick up their heels in sequined thongs and little else, the thin beauties slinking down the Champs-Élysées might wear next to nothing beneath their fashionable garb, but Micki and I would be demurely swathed in a square yard of cotton each. No need to worry about any indiscretions with French men, Jeff.....

When I ran errands in the last days before our departure, I discovered that Micki had been everywhere and seen everyone before me. Walking to the post office, I met our pastor's wife, Mila, who was getting out of her car.

"All ready for the big trip?" she asked.

"You've been talking to Micki!" I deduced. Sure enough, they had recently worked a funeral together.

Then I went to the bank to get cash and make sure my debit card was set up for the travel abroad. The teller, Marcia, greeted me.

"Micki was just in here! She's so excited."

Which I could believe, because I was excited, and I'd already been to Europe a zillion times, including twice to Paris. Micki's last pre-trip email revealed her eagerness:

I just have a few last-minute things to throw in the suitcase, otherwise I'm ready to roll!!! I still can't believe this is happening. You might need to smack me a few times in case I'm speechless, when we get there. I know—me speechless would be something to see!!

Finally, the preparations ended, the final hours ticked by, and just seven weeks after Vacation Bible School and the prospect of a typical summer, we were ready to leave for France.

2
Endurance Test

It's too bad the travel experience has to be spoiled by the actual travel. Trip preparation is a giddy joy, in-country sightseeing a delicious pleasure, and rosy-hued memories a sweet, delirious dream. But physically getting from Point A at home to Point B abroad is a grueling, boring marathon of hurry-up-and-wait, of cramped spaces and knotted muscles and grumpy sleeplessness, of too hot or too cold, and most of it compounded by irritating tourists.

I'm never more misanthropic than when I travel. It makes me surly, unpleasant, not fit for human interaction. That's a ridiculous paradox, I know—leave home to meet new people, see new things, and then despise the other tourists, their loud conversations, their massive, oversized luggage, their huge butts waddling four abreast and blocking pedestrian traffic flow, their inane questions, their insistence on talking with strangers who would rather read, thank you very much. Not all tourists offend on these counts, of course, but the ones who do loom large in their presence and overpower awareness of quieter, more considerate, knowledgeable, and mindful travelers. The meek may inherit the earth, but the obnoxious rule at the airport.

It didn't used to be like this. In its heyday, air travel was something special, and those lucky enough to experience it lived up to its image. (At least they did according to the old movies and news clips I've seen.) Flying was glamorous, a great adventure, with people carefully dressing up in sharp suits and ties, sophisticated skirts and jackets. They looked their best, acted their best. They were classy. But today? Not anymore. Budget air travel doesn't rank far above bus travel these days, and that's reflected in the way people dress. Airline expenditures have been cut to the bone, ticket prices are relatively affordable, and every Tom, Dick, and Harry can travel overseas in their sloppy sweatpants.

Including me.

Up to our departure time, our trip to France was still all glorious possibility, and the prevailing emotion was excitement, not irritation. Our flight wasn't until late Sunday afternoon, so my family and I went to church in the morning. During coffee time after the service, Micki and I were showered with good wishes for our trip. John and Jeff, our patient husbands, stoically waited while we chatted with—it seemed—nearly every member of our congregation, many of whom expressed a quiet envy.

Promptly at 1:30, Micki tossed her bags into our van for our ride to the airport. As we backed away from her house to leave, Jeff stood next to the driveway and pretended to weep, wiping his eyes with exaggerated gestures. He was very good-natured about our departure, considering he was sure to miss Micki. Maybe it helped that she had fixed a big family dinner after church, a final act of love and support before she left. She had probably packed a freezer full of home-cooked meals for when we were gone, too. My family, by contrast, had lunched on three frozen dinners and one frozen burrito, all microwaved, and my husband had requested a good supply of cereal to sustain them while I was gone.

We arrived at the airport three hours before our flight, unsure whether to follow the guidelines to check in four hours early for an international flight, or just two hours, because our first leg was domestic, to Detroit. Micki and I are both careful planners, and both cautious about making sure we have all our bases covered, all our ducks in a row. There was no way we would risk losing our seats because we checked in too late. The bigger risk we would run was arriving before the airline personnel.

As it was, three hours was surely a safe compromise, because when we checked in, we were the only passengers in the hall. There were three workers behind the Delta counter, but they chatted among themselves and ignored us, so we went to the self-check kiosk to see what that involved, a novel experience for me. We swiped our passports and confirmed who we were, then it printed out our boarding passes, much to my surprise and delight.

As far as we could tell, the Delta staff was just standing around shooting the breeze and couldn't be bothered by a couple of passengers. Those passengers still had suitcases to unload, however, so we tentatively advanced to the counter, unsure whether we should interrupt the workers. It seemed rude, when they were so busy ignoring us. But the women greeted us very pleasantly, checked our luggage, and commented on our going "all the way" to France. They made it sound like a truly exotic, far-flung destination, like Timbuktu or Tierra del Fuego rather than Paris, probably the top tourist destination in the world. But as far as they knew, this was a once-in-a-lifetime trip for us, something we'd dreamed of since Girl Scout days, had finally achieved, and would never venture again. Maybe they had dreamed of the same thing— and still were.

I've never understood that mentality, that wistful wishing for a European trip by people who think they'll never go. As a type of travel writer, I hear not infrequently from people, "Oh, I wish I could go there someday." Well, why don't you? I know that finances keep many would-be travelers close to home for their entire lives, or health restrictions do, but the ones who clearly have the resources to travel, what's keeping them away from their dreams? It's not terribly difficult to travel in Europe. The language barriers, the money systems, the social differences—none of those are insurmountable. And if people don't enjoy planning their own trips (a concept so foreign to me that I struggle to accept it), they can sign up for a packaged tour. What could be easier?! You show up with your money and your luggage, and everything else is done for you. As independent as I am, I admit there are times when I'm trudging on foot through rainy streets to see sights, and an organized bus tour sounds pretty attractive. If only it weren't for the other tourists....

Now, my husband has a real excuse for not traveling more than he does. He doesn't like it. The long flight, the time change, the complete disorientation and upsetting of his routine all throw him off his game—and his sleep patterns—for weeks. We've reached the peaceful agreement that he's happier at home, and I'm just fine traveling with other companions. Such as Micki.

Relieved of our suitcases and saddled with just our backpacks and enormous tote bags, we trekked toward the main hall of the terminal. It was time to take the ceremonial "Waiting In the Airport For Our First Flight" photo that would start my trip photo album, as similar photos do every album I create to document my travels. Micki and I are happy and excited in our picture, ready to begin our adventure. I have to laugh at the contrast between us. I'm wearing a moss green shirt dubiously enlivened by a silk scarf of muddy green, red, brown, and deep purple. My dark hair is straight, pulled back from my pale face in a clip. Micki's shirt is a bright mix of sky blue and fuschia with a deep vee neck that reveals a lacy, hot-pink camisole underneath. She is blond and tan and wears large gold hoop earrings. My ears are bare.

08/08/2010

Micki and I wait in Cedar Rapids for our flight to Detroit.

My previous "Off to France" photos are remarkably similar, and not just because they're taken in the same airport, quite possibly in the same seats. On my first Paris trip, with my grandmother, I'm uncharacteristically cheery in a dark pink sweater and a light silk scarf, but my grandmother fills in on darks for me, with her black sweater. This was a thrilling visit for both of us, our first (and her last) to France. I'm holding our boarding passes in front of us, grinning.

By my second "Waiting to Fly to France" picture, with my daughter, I'd reverted to form and am wearing a black shirt under a moss green jacket adorned with a dark scarf. (I always take scarves to France. The French are famously gaga about scarves.) In this photo, eight-year-old Emily stands next to me, holding a large blond doll. The reflective straps of her backpack glow eerily in the camera's flash. At the edge of the picture, one each of her brother's arms and legs intrude, a welcome reminder that here at the airport was also the four-year-old sweetheart who hadn't even existed at the time of that first France trip. And, by the time of the Micki trip, he was seven.

With the required trip-commencement photos snapped, I hugged my family goodbye. They left to investigate a nearby mini-golf course, which would keep them in the area for a while in case any problems arose with our flight. I felt quite cutting-edge being able to check in with John throughout my airport waits, flipping open my 2007-era cell phone, while scores of Bluetooth mumblers scurried past us. Yes, I'm a technology dinosaur, one who wants a phone so I can make phone calls. Not schedule appointments. Not take pictures. Not surf the Web. Certainly not to text.

But even my Paleolithic technology was a huge improvement over most of my previous trips. In my dark, pre-cellular days, I could only contact my family if they were at home and my AT&T calling card had credits on it. I would locate an actual phone booth and enter the appropriate toll-free number, enter my card's code of twelve digits, and then enter the complete phone number I was calling, including a 1 and the area code. I rarely pecked in all thirty-four digits without messing up and having to start over, so I especially appreciated the ease and accuracy of being able to call John on the mini-golf course from the comfort of my airport chair, by pushing just two buttons, one to search and one to call.

Micki and I soon left the atrium-like central waiting area at the airport to find our gate, so we could easily keep track of any updates that might be posted about our flight. Our foresight proved fortunate, because our flight *was* moved to a different gate. In the mighty Eastern Iowa Airport, that meant shifting to the next seating area, perhaps forty feet from where we were.

At our new gate, we could see a problem with our inbound plane, which stood outside the window. The deplaning process was held up because the crew could not remove a heavy automated wheelchair from the belly of the plane. We watched through the window as a group of six workers shifted the chair one way, and then another, trying to fit it through the rigid hatch. In the meantime, the passengers were trapped on board the plane, not allowed to leave until the motorized chair was safely extricated. I imagined that Stephen Hawking was aboard, patiently waiting for his chair to restore his mobility, perhaps calculating the rate of solar radiation that was striking the plane on that sunny day. The airport workers continued to wrestle delicately with the chair, eventually finding the right angle to ease its bulk through the opening and lower it carefully to the ground. Flush with success (they actually cheered, as I recall), they unfolded it and buzzed it out of the way, to be reunited with its owner. Once the obstacle of the chair was removed, everything progressed quickly, and we were soon able to board.

We had watched the drama of the chair removal with a certain interest and impatience, but no particular anxiety. As delays went, it was barely a blip compared to the delay Emily and I had experienced trying to fly to Paris in late February 2007. Winter flights are always a gamble in the snow states, and this one cost us, despite trying to outwit it.

I had planned a French research trip with young Emily, easily justifying a week's missed school because of the all the culture and history she would be exposed to. I even made her research and report on important topics before we left, so she would be guaranteed an educational experience, at least up to the point we visited Disney Paris. She read short biographies of Marie Antoinette and Napoleon. She investigated artworks she would see at the Orsay and Louvre museums, along with the artists behind them, and discovered a particular interest in Degas and his ballet dancers. Emily was prepared. Our itinerary was prepared. Our Paris lodging and transportation plans were prepared. Everything was in place to squeeze the most out of our scant six days in France.

But Mother Nature threatened to derail the whole experience. Our flight was scheduled for a Saturday. On Friday, ominous reports of impending ice storms hit the news. If the ice arrived on schedule, we would be stranded in our tiny northeast Iowa town Saturday morning, almost two hours away from the airport under *normal* driving conditions. With ice on the roads, we might as well be in the Yukon. Once the weather predictions turned dire on Friday, I called John at work early in the afternoon, asking him to come home ahead of schedule. I finished packing, and when I picked Emily up from her school at the end of the day, she found the whole family in the van, ready to drive straight to a hotel in Cedar Rapids. Our trip might still be threatened by the weather, but we would at least make it as far as the airport!

The next morning, John and Paul dropped us off for our flight hours before we needed to be there. The ice storm was roaring across Iowa now, and they were going to try to beat it home. They didn't, but they did eventually arrive safely back in Shell Rock. Emily and I were also affected by the ice. Our flight to Chicago was delayed indefinitely, but unlike many others, it was not yet cancelled. Eventually, there was a brief window of opportunity. We were able to board, and after extensive de-icing of the plane, we departed. The storm was hitting a slew of states in the Upper Midwest, though, not just Iowa, and we arrived to absolute bedlam at Chicago O'Hare, two hours behind schedule, late enough that we missed our flight to France.

As we stood in the endless line to reschedule our flight, I looked around at the hordes of fellow stranded passengers and wondered where we would spend the night. Could I find a safe spot to sleep on the floor with my diabetic daughter and our luggage? I knew that sleep was not really an option for me under those circumstances, but I still needed a safe place to nest with her.

Those concerns occupied me during our hour-long wait to speak with an agent. As we slowly shuffled forward, I dreaded the prospect of spending the night on the hard floor with thousands of other stranded travelers. We were rescued from my fears, however, by the friendly airline agent who worked with us. She booked us in the last two seats available on the next day's flight to Paris, *and* booked us into a local hotel at a reduced rate. I felt we'd been given a great gift as we went in search of the shuttle bus that would carry us to the Hyatt Regency. We wouldn't have to spend the night at the airport, on the floor, among strangers. Everything looked possible.

Although we had arrived at O'Hare around 3:30, by the time we headed outside for the shuttle, it was dark and snowing heavily. But we reached the hotel with no problems, checked in, went to our lovely room, and after a few phone calls, we went to bed. We ended up losing our first pre-paid night in Paris but were happy to have escaped the major winter storm with only one day's delay.

Micki's and my situation was much less nerve-racking. Good weather kept us basically on schedule the whole trip. After the bulky, heavy wheelchair was removed from the plane in Cedar Rapids, we were able to board the small jet, stuffing our backpacks—with some effort—into the narrow confines of the storage bins above our heads. The routineness of the boarding, the ordinariness of it, was almost a letdown after traveling with Emily, though. That Cedar Rapids-to-Chicago flight was the first time she was aware of being on a plane, and her wide-eyed excitement—along with the doll she had tucked in her arm—consistently drew comments from the airline crew. The flight attendant who greeted us at the plane asked Emily what the name of her doll was (Jillian) and whether it was her (Jillian's) first flight. The attendant then let us enter the cockpit to meet the pilots, who asked the same questions and let us take a picture of them there with Emily and the doll. Traveling with an eager eight-year-old girl opened doors throughout that trip that two middle-aged women couldn't quite pull off three years later.

Rather than transferring in Chicago, Micki and I would change planes in Detroit, which was fine with me, because I like the Detroit airport, with its underground light show on the tunneled walk between terminals. We wanted to get to our next gate as quickly as we could (best to be early!), so we

Emily visits the cockpit on our way to France.

trotted along the moving sidewalks, burdened like burros with our backpacks and overstuffed tote bag "purses." We made it to the gate just in time to call our guys and hit the restrooms before boarding.

We were flying Air France, which resulted in a fancy French menu for supper, despite our cheap seats in the back of the plane. Micki had white wine with her meal. I had champagne and, just for a moment, a glimpse of the glamour that formerly distinguished international travel. But reality quickly slammed into us as we ate our foil- and cellophane-wrapped food on our tiny tray tables with our elbows wedged against our sides. We were a couple of fleshy praying mantises pinned to our seats, stubby arms waving helplessly about, trying to wield a plastic knife and fork. I desperately wanted to move my feet around but couldn't, as any attempt to readjust resulted in kicking against the metal box under the seat in front of me. As if air passenger space weren't limited enough, the airline took up much of the foot room with these bulky boxes, which we assumed housed the electronics of the individual video players we each had, attached to the seat back in front of us. Whatever the boxes had in them, they were unbudgable space hogs, and we hated them.

We had our choice of several movies and TV shows on our private screens. To start off, though, we needed to choose the language we wanted on the menu page. We both selected English, but the program took a while to load. During the delay, Micki pressed the language button again and converted herself back to French. She chased the English option for another round or two, but eventually she caught it. Rather than try to watch a show, I chose to display the flight progress screen, to follow the little airplane as it made its way from Detroit to Paris on a map. That was just for occasional reference; my real entertainment was reading.

Soon after we ate, the lights dimmed and the flight

attendants had everyone shut their window shades. Because the plane was only half full, I was able to move to the two empty seats in front of us, so Micki and I each had a window and an aisle seat to get comfortable in. In theory we could, anyway. Our plan to sprawl across two seats to catch some sleep was thwarted by the design of the plane. First, there was no place to put our feet, because of the damnable equipment boxes, and second, the arm rests between the two seats were firmly anchored in place and could not be raised up out of the way. The French may have perfected the art of sleeping upright with motionless feet squeezed together on the floor before them, mermaid-like, but that skill eluded Micki and me. We each fidgeted in our short row of seats, searching in vain for a comfortable resting spot. Eventually, monotony and travel medication combined to usher in a light doze.

Until a baby's screams rent the air.

We had seen the family of three when they boarded after we did and tried to seat themselves in *another* family's seats, because they were dissatisfied with theirs. The mother of the baby was vocally unhappy and demanding, but the flight attendant made them return to their own seats and relinquish the ones they had tried to take over. If the baby's cries were that mother's revenge on the family they had tried to displace, then she more than succeeded in punishing them.

The baby didn't just cry; it screamed. Nonstop. For hours on end. By the time people began raising their window shades and the fresh sunshine burst in, the chic, red-haired *maman* was looking decidedly worse for the wear. The rest of us may have had to put up with the piercing wails of the baby, but *she* had had to deal with her unhappy infant *and* the unspoken hostility that emanated in thick waves from the rest of the cabin.

I rejoined Micki in our assigned seats and observed that my little plane tracker showed us flying off the coast of Ireland.

Time to eat again. Our French breakfast was nowhere near as good as our French dinner had been. Wine and champagne were replaced by plain yogurt, and we could only choke down a few bites. Unsweetened, unfruited yogurt was simply too dietarily wholesome for our Midwestern palates, accustomed as we were to regarding Jello with marshmallows as a salad. We were soon approaching Paris, however, and the baby recommenced her howling for our descent. We landed uneventfully, the baby quieted, and we, like most of the other passengers, rose to cram into the aisle and assemble our various bags while we waited for the signal to deplane.

Getting from the plane to the main terminal at Charles de Gaulle airport was a labyrinthine nightmare in our sleep-deprived state. Like ungainly cattle being driven through a series of chutes, the herd left the plane and entered a maze of corridors, escalators, blind corners, and gaping halls to get to a shuttle bus. The bus then hauled us, bleary-eyed and stumbling at every shift of the vehicle, across the tarmac to the main building, where another bracing hike brought us to the luggage carousel. We retrieved our suitcases and then, luggage in hand or strapped to our bodies, on our own for the first time, we truly started our French experience.

I'd known I would be mentally and physically exhausted when we arrived, with the energy and brain power of a soft-boiled egg (honestly, my legs felt just as quivery), so I had written out on an index card everything we had to do that first day, starting with "Find ATM" in the airport. We wandered much of the terminal before we saw one, discovering in the process that the term I had learned for ATM in French— *DAB*—drew uncomprehending stares. Oh! You mean *un distributeur*! So, asking periodically, *Où est un distributeur?* and following the general gesturing that accompanied each answer (people couldn't help turning to look in the direction we needed to go), we eventually tracked one down.

I arrived in France with no more than 20 euros on me (less than $30), leftover from a previous trip. As such, I was profoundly relieved when the *distributeur* obediently spit out colorful bills for me. Then Micki tried her cash card, and the ATM rejected it. Every time she tried to use it, which was several, her request was denied. This was not the welcome to France that Micki had hoped for, but I assured her that since my card worked, we'd be fine. (And after Micki had Jeff talk with their bank, her card did work later in the trip.)

At the airport's tourist information office, we got our Paris transportation passes and our museum passes, which would simplify our visit considerably because we wouldn't have to buy any tickets to travel or see things. Then we wandered to the trains, wheeling our suitcases behind us, tired eyes darting wearily, warily, to and fro as we scoured the concourse for potential pickpockets. My legs dragged with exhaustion, and every now and then, one of my knees buckled, threatening to send me tumbling to the floor. After a little dip, though, I managed to catch myself with the other leg, which was steady for the moment. I made it through that first, sleepless day in Paris at a steady trudge, punctuated by an occasional random curtsey.

We boarded our train for Paris, slumped in our seats with our bags tight against us, waited fifteen minutes until the train departed, then followed the blue line on the map as we passed through numerous graffiti-enhanced Paris suburbs. Although both the métro diagram on the train and the more detailed version on my Paris map omitted a number of the stops, we were able to track our progress well enough and exit with no problem at the proper stop, despite our load of luggage. Searching for our connection in the confusion of tunnels, we passed a man working at an information table. We asked him how to get to RER line C, which we would take for a few stops before hopping on another line for a stop or two.

It's a good thing we asked, because line C was closed for repairs in the section we needed. Fortunately, the métro system in Paris is so extensive that it was easy to find another route to the area we wanted, and we soon alighted by a McDonald's down the street from where we needed to be. I was happy that Micki elected to walk the distance to our hotel rather than switch lines for one stop, because the walk would take us by the Champ de Mars, where we would see the Eiffel Tower looming over the huge, grassy lawn. That first breathtaking view of the *Tour Eiffel* made it official— we really were in Paris. We were tired. We were grubby. We were loaded with luggage that branded us from blocks away as tourists, but we were in Paris.

We clomped to our hotel, checked in ahead of schedule, and quickly cleaned up from the flight. Micki, I was pleased to discover, did not share Emily's disappointment with our room in that hotel. Like most Paris hotel rooms, it was small,

08/11/2010

The Champ de Mars park as seen from the Eiffel Tower. We dragged our suitcases across the far end on the way to our hotel.

and Emily's response after our unplanned stay at the Hyatt Regency the night before had been, "Oh. Is this it?" She was tremendously let down after the generous size and luxury in Chicago, which was ironic, because I'd deliberately chosen a nicer hotel in a safe residential district to house my daughter (and later, Micki). It had a telephone! It had a TV! There had been no riots nearby in the recent past!

How would Emily have responded if I'd taken her to the spartan hotel in the Latin Quarter that my grandmother and I had lodged in? Her privileged little nose would undoubtedly have sniffed with even greater disdain. Micki would have handled it just fine, I realized later, and perhaps would have preferred its student and multi-cultural liveliness to the sedate safety of the rue Cler neighborhood. But I'd played it safe on this first trip together, and we thoroughly enjoyed our air conditioning and modern bathroom before heading out to experience the city of so many dreams.

3
Time Travel

The problem with American flights to Europe—besides their length—is their timing. Planes almost always land early in the morning, leaving the whole day to soldier through when a traveler is sleep-deprived and disoriented. It may suit the schedule of a packaged tour to cram a day's sights in before sleeping in Europe, but not me. I'd prefer to arrive just in time for bed. Unfortunately, that's usually not an option, at least for us coach travelers.

After Micki and I checked into our hotel and cleaned up for the day, we ventured into Paris, starting with the very heart of the city: the Île de la Cité (the "island of the city"). Paris is thought to have originated on this island in the Seine, inhabited by Celtic tribes since the third century B.C. It was a desirable spot to settle in, in those days (still is): easy to cross the river there, but the island was also easy to defend against invaders. One of the Celtic tribes, the Parisii, lived on the island around the time of Julius Caesar's reign (ca. 52 B.C.), and from them comes the name *Paris*.

I suppose it's just as well that Micki and I were groggy

The official center of Paris (where distances are measured from) is marked by a metal disk in front of Notre-Dame Cathedral on the Île de la Cité, the oldest part of the city.

and exhausted that first day in France. It made everything that much more surreal, so unlike the steady, predictable life we knew. We were obviously suffering the jet lag of flying across seven time zones. It's more fun, though, to think that we were simultaneously traveling seven hours into the future (compared to our home base back in the Midwest), but also centuries into the past, and in a sense we were. We were surrounded by the buildings, the streets, the bridges of French history. It wasn't like at home, where hundreds of years earlier, everything around us would have been prairie or woodland or wetland, populated only by wild animals and native tribes. Here, in Paris, *things happened.* And here was solid evidence of those earlier times, down virtually every street. Built of stone, built to last.

How much history had played out on these very sites? How much blood spilled in these gutters? (How much waste dumped into those self-same gutters? The stench must have been unbearable.) Everywhere we went, everywhere we looked, were the ghosts of history, because we knew, *we felt,* that we were walking the same streets, seeing the same buildings, that

so many historical figures had. That Marie Curie had. That
Victor Hugo had. Picasso. Monet. Renoir. Rodin. Dumas.
Napoleon. Robespierre. Marie Antoinette. Louis XIV. Heloïse
and Abélard. Maybe they wouldn't recognize all of present-
day Paris, but surely they would know much of it, especially
in the ancient city center.

Notre-Dame Cathedral squats right there on the Île de la
Cité, if a building can both squat and soar. It's very tall and
grand, but just so solid, so massive. It hunkers at the east end
of the island like a defensive lineman waiting for the ball snap.
And it's old, started way back in 1163 and completed by 1345.
An impressive hulk of French Gothic architecture, it leads to
the inevitable question (as all these old, massive structures
do), *How did they do it?* How did the laborers construct such
a large, high, complicated structure without the benefit of
our modern lifting, cutting, and measuring equipment? The
practical achievement of assembling this huge and beautiful
edifice—one that has withstood numerous assaults and in-
dignities over the ages—is simply mind-boggling, as anyone
who has ever attempted a home-improvement project should
be able to appreciate.

The French Revolution was not kind to Notre-Dame.
Some 28 kingly statues on the front façade—biblical kings,
mind you—were beheaded in the mistaken belief that they
represented French kings. But Christian statues and paintings were plundered or destroyed too, and the great building
ended up as a food warehouse for a while. Later, its fortunes
improved and Napoleon crowned himself emperor here.
Notre-Dame, though, is not only historically significant, but
architecturally so. It was one of the first buildings to use flying buttresses, those gracefully arched exterior supports that
help keep the outer walls of a structure from bulging outward
(or even collapsing) from the weight of the roof. I read that
the exterior of the building was originally brightly colored,

Notre-Dame Cathedral

but I was unable to visualize that. Notre-Dame is such a staid and serious natural stone color now, as befits its dignity and importance. It was originally tarted up like a Mexican restaurant?? Inconceivable.

The line to enter Notre-Dame on this day stretched the length of the large square before it, perhaps a full city block. I'd never seen any line to enter the cathedral before, but then, I'd never been to Paris in the summer before, so I was in for numerous surprises.

Too impatient to wait (and in danger of falling asleep if we stopped moving), we bypassed Notre-Dame and crossed a bridge to the neighboring Île St. Louis, the second historic island in the middle of the city. We spied a shop's service window along the street and promptly ordered ice cream, lemon for me and peach for Micki. Cones in hand, we leisurely wandered back behind Notre-Dame and then on to the Latin Quarter. We strolled past bookseller stalls and narrow, crooked buildings shoehorned into every conceivable gap and crevice along the narrow, crooked medieval lanes. Spaces so tight that they would house only garbage cans in an American city were here home to highly vertical *buildings*, one small room wide but several stories high. And I would love to know the stories behind them.

I had another brush with the city's ghosts here—imagining the former scholars and academics striding around, robes flying open behind them, conversing in the Latin language that gave this quarter its name. Or, on a fictional front, was this the area where D'Artagnan (the so-called fourth musketeer) rented his rooms when he arrived in Paris from Gascony? I couldn't remember. There is just so much history in Paris. So much rich possibility for flights of fancy.

After our quick introduction to the city center, we searched for métro line 4 and rode it to the base of the hill where Sacré-Coeur Basilica stands. The area was a warren of streets, a chaos of commercialism—teeming with tourists and lined with

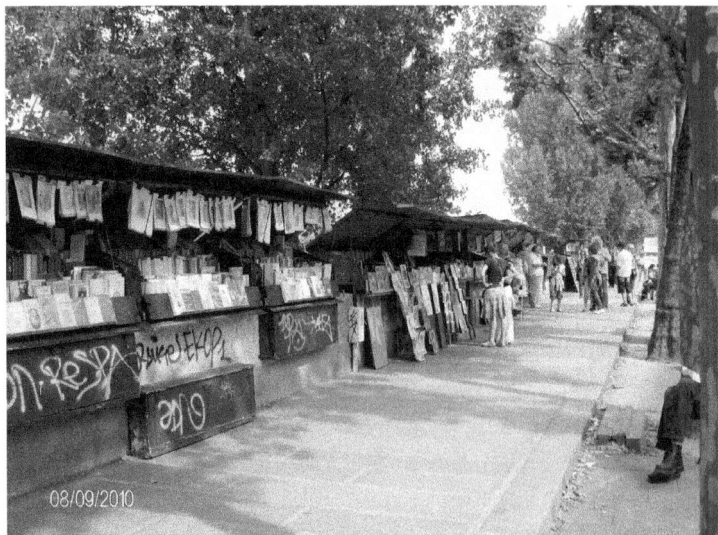

Art and bookseller stalls along the Seine River

cheesy shops of cheap junk. I clamped my tote bag tightly against my side, alert to possible pickpockets in the crowd. Sacré-Coeur, milky white, loomed above us on an impressively high hill, the highest spot in Paris. Fortunately, our métro passes covered rides on the funicular, and unlike on my trip with Emily, it was actually functioning this day. Having hauled myself up the 230 or so steps to the top of Montmartre on the previous trip, I had already done the martyr act and was more than happy to wait a few minutes for a ride up.

Also unlike my earlier visit (which was at night), the church was open, and we entered to view its Byzantine interior. The basilica is a relative baby compared to Notre-Dame. It wasn't started until 1870 and wasn't finished until 1914. It's actually modern, although you wouldn't know it by looking at it. At least, I wouldn't. There was a mass in progress when we were there, and I thought how strange it must be to have your local church also be a huge tourist attraction. How can you have a meaningful service with hundreds of strangers milling about, gaping and taking pictures? Obviously, this devout group had far greater religious focus than I did.

The hilly Montmartre district has been associated with artists and general degenerateness since the early 1800s. (That's where the famous Moulin Rouge dance hall is. You know— high-kicking can-can dancers, exposed flesh.) We walked to the Place du Tertre, a crowded square with artists set up by the dozen, painting the likenesses of tourists for a fee. Knowing Micki likes to shop, I was surprised that she didn't even slow down. After a loop through the famous square, we returned to the basilica. One of my guidebooks—*Eyewitness: France*— points out a church right across the street from Sacré-Coeur, called St-Pierre de Montmartre. The book notes that this church has "origins dating back to the 6th century." That's the 500s—up to 1500 years ago! What is an American supposed to do with a date like that? How are we supposed to process it?? Anything that predates the American Revolution tends to be a bit hazy in my understanding of history. I can place the dates on a timeline, but can't really *comprehend* them.

We stood a while in the small square before the basilica, admiring Paris laid out at our feet, then descended the series of terraces back toward our métro stop. On the way, we had to fend off trinket salesmen and, in particular, friendship bracelet hustlers. Fortunately, I had read about the latter before we left and was prepared for their tricks. They basically capture the wrist of an unwary passerby and, demonstrating their craft, quickly weave a bracelet on the tourist's arm. The finished product won't come off, so the vendors pressure people to pay for an item they didn't want or request. They tried hard to get us, one after another, a gauntlet of bracelet braiders. I know I had to shake at least one off from my arm, jerking

Sacré-Coeur Basilica

away and barking a sharp *non!* In my memory, I even elbowed them away, but I'm probably elaborating there. In hindsight, I realize that the trinket hustlers were probably all immigrants, struggling to make a living, but we really didn't want the junk they were pushing, and their aggressiveness set off a defensive reaction in us. We just wanted to get away.

Tired at the end of a very long couple of days with precious little sleep, we rode the métro to our "home" stop. We surfaced right at our neighborhood grocery store, bought bread and apples and returned to the hotel. We ate on the beds and called our husbands to assure them that we had arrived safely and all was going well. Well, mostly going well. We were having some problems with our métro passes, but surely those were taken care of (as I'll get to shortly).

Cozy in our room with all its modern conveniences, we turned away from ancient Paris, away from our miles of walking, away from our sleepless plane ride. After two endless days, it was finally night, and we collapsed into bed.

4
What's That Stick?

Our second day in Paris started out much as the first one had—a beautiful day, and our métro passes (the ones that were supposed to save us so much time and trouble) didn't work right. It reached the point that we were reluctant to ride the métro, because we knew that one or the other of us (although, oddly, hardly ever both of us) would have trouble with our transportation pass.

To enter the métro system, we would feed the card with its magnetized strip through a turnstile, pluck it up where it popped out, and pass through a gate, which snapped shut after each ticket holder. Thus, sometimes the first of us would make it to the train side of the barriers. Then the second person would feed a card through, but all too often it would be rejected by the turnstile reader with the message displayed, *non valuble*. The common result was that we had one of us trapped on one side of the gate (with a card that could not be re-used at the same stop for a certain length of time), and the other trapped on the *other* side of the gate, unable to gain access. This first happened on our very first foray out after finding our hotel room—my brand-new, perfectly valid métro ticket was spit back out at me. I walked to the nearby ticket window, explained my trouble, and the worker replaced my ticket, no problem.

Until it happened again. And again. And then it happened to Micki a couple of times. Then to me. And then her. The whole process became a routine to us. If the first one of us had a ticket refused, we could fix the problem together, but often one of us was on the métro side of the barrier, while the other one fumed and stomped to the sales window to get a replacement. Micki accomplished this very effectively by shoving her ticket under the glass partition and rapping out, "Not working." The workers must spend half their days replacing these métro passes for tourists, because no one batted an eye.

By the time I was receiving my fifth pass, I finally asked the worker in frustration, "Why does this keep happening?"

"You need to keep zuh card away from zuh magnet," he explained with a charming French accent. "Even a credeet card can be a prublem."

Oh....! The light dawned. I had been storing my pass in the same easily accessible interior pocket that I kept my sunglass clip in, and my sunglass clip attached to my glasses with... a fairly powerful little magnet. Micki's problems stemmed from her high-security, steel-cabled document bag. It had strong magnets to help keep the middle section closed. And where did she keep her métro pass? In the middle section, of course, the most convenient one.

Our second day started with more métro pass mishaps (our problem wasn't diagnosed until that afternoon), but we eventually made it to the Latin Quarter, intending to catch Notre-Dame before the crowd hit. Already at nine there was a line of tourists waiting to enter, but it was much shorter than it had been the previous day, and it moved very quickly. The majestic building with its huge flying buttresses demands a certain respect, even awe. We entered the dim interior, admired the rose windows, and sat a moment on stark wooden benches to absorb the dusky atmosphere. We would have liked to climb to the bell tower, but even early in the day, that line was dauntingly long. My close encounter with a rooftop gargoyle would have to wait for a future trip.

After our quick tour of the cathedral, we walked to nearby Sainte-Chapelle, famous for its brilliant stained-glass windows. While a beautiful and interesting chapel, it beats me how the many windows were used to tell Bible stories to people who couldn't read (as one of our guidebooks informed us), when it was hard even to see the scenes on them, with their soaring heights and tiny shards of colored glass.

While Micki dutifully examined the artistic wonders before us, I was more taken with a sign at the top of the stone spiral staircase we had ascended to reach the heavenly upper

The beautiful stained-glass windows of Sainte-Chapelle

level: inside a yellow warning triangle, a stick-like figure was shown tripping and falling over a low rectangular block that I assumed represented a step. Or, perhaps the floors of the chapel were so uneven that stumbling and pitching headlong to the floor were a real threat. The words next to the image stated "RISQUE DE TREBUCHEMENT," which translated easily enough to "risk of" and then something that must be related to trebuchet, something like a catapult.

Warning sign in the chapel

I was highly amused by the juxtaposition of the sublime beauty of the chapel and the garish road sign warning us not to catapult ourselves by tripping. But it must be said that France, as other European countries, has countless uneven walking surfaces and endless opportunity for stumbling. If they were placed in the U.S., half the French walkways and tourist sites would be marked as hazardous—probably painted a bright yellow—and very likely shut off from visitors entirely because of the potential danger. Micki and I did not linger in the chapel, but while we were there, I did not see a single person trip up *or* down the stairs or otherwise fall, so the sign was doing its job.

On we walked to the Conciergerie, former palace, former prison. Again, I was struck by the crowds, by how many more people were jammed in than when I had visited these same places with Emily in late winter. Clothing practices were also wildly different than before. There was great diversity in what people wore, not the standard black as far as the eye could see. We saw jeans, shorts, nylon track suits, bright colors and patterns. We also saw the ever-popular light neck scarves, however, on women and some men, so we knew that we were, indeed, still in Paris. But the rest of the clothing baffled me. Were the rules that relaxed in August, European vacation month? Do Parisians cut loose in the summer, or were these all other tourists we were seeing? People were even smiling in public, visibly having a good time! (That decided it; they must have been tourists.) We could still pick out obvious Americans, though, with their white shoes, baggy denim shorts, and ball caps, even among the uncommonly bright garb.

We ate lunch in the courtyard at the foot of the Tuileries, right by the Louvre, where we each got the day's special of a chicken sandwich, a Coke Light, and an apple tart from "Pauls" food cart. We found a bit of low wall in the shade to sit on, with a fine view of garden statues and other tourists also sitting and eating. The pigeons were a pain, edging close in search of crumbs. It didn't help that other tourists were feeding them, giving them encouragement. Or maybe it did help, keeping them away from us. By the time we finished our sandwiches, we were too full for the apple tarts, so Micki carried them in her daypack as we continued up the Champs-Élysées.

*****

Paris, as everyone knows, is notorious for having snooty, unfriendly citizens. Also unfriendly are most postal workers I've encountered in other large foreign cities. Thus, I expected Parisian postal workers to take bureaucratic unfriendliness to new heights. But Micki and I needed postcard stamps to America, so we braved the bureaucratic dragons and popped

into the post office on the Champs-Élysées. The post office
was practically empty, and the woman working was extremely
nice, without a hint of snootiness. I couldn't help wondering,
was she the regular Paris worker, or a friendly provincial filling in during the vacation month? A native French person
would have known immediately by her accent, of course, but
I was lucky to understand *anything* in French, forget identifying a regional accent.

With stamps and postcards in hand, we headed to a nearby McDonald's to buy overpriced drinks and write postcards
home. We wanted to send them early in the trip, to make sure
they arrived while we were gone.

McDonald's was packed, filled with French people and
tourists. I waited in line at least ten minutes to order our two
moyen (medium) Coke Lights. At about $4.50 each. With no
ice. (Free refills?? Don't make me laugh!) But the drinks gave
us an excuse to linger on tippy bar stools at an eating counter
at the front window, where we could look down the sidewalk
of the Champs-Élysées and watch the kaleidoscopic parade of
tourists, shoppers, and beggars. And, as tippy and cramped
as our bar stools were, they were highly desirable, even in the
middle of the afternoon. Micki had had to fend off people who
wanted our seats while she was waiting (and waiting and waiting) for me to get the Cokes. Once I got there and we started
writing our postcards, we thought it would be wise to use the
bathroom before we left, so we took turns for that, too. While
she was gone, *I* had to shoo away people who wanted *her* bar
stool. By the time we finished our postcards and packed up
to leave, people were hovering around just waiting to swoop
in for our spots. I sympathized with them, because I would
have done the same thing.

As we had worked our way up the Champs-Élysées, that
famous shopping street, we had bought nothing but our
stamps. However, we had noticed a Swarovski crystal store

near the McDonalds and, after our break, we made a beeline there. It was fabulously bling-y, crystals blinking everywhere under the lights. Even the stairs to the second floor were imbedded with crystals so both the tread and the riser gleamed and sparkled with them. Micki saw a necklace and earrings she really liked, and I saw a green crystal charm that I knew Emily would like, but it was the start of our visit and we were frugal and didn't buy anything.

We continued up the hill to the Arc de Triomphe. Because of our museum passes, we were able to bypass the depressingly long line for tickets and proceed directly to the much shorter line to enter the stairs. We pitied the multitude that had to wait so long, but were also smugly satisfied that we had been so smart as to get those convenient passes. (There was no magnetic strip on the museum passes, so they were functioning beautifully for us.) Girding our loins, we entered the stairway and started the climb. We heaved ourselves up the

Arc de Triomphe

tight spiral staircase, muscles burning with each step. About the time my legs were going to flame out, I stepped to the side to catch my breath, only to discover on reentering the spiral that we were on the final twist before it emptied into a museum. We crossed the room, looked briefly at the displays, and then continued on to the next level of stairs. I read that there are 284 steps to get to the top, but I didn't count them. I needed all my breath just to climb.

Touring European sites of a vertical nature is an ordeal bordering on a health risk for many of us Americans. I was heavy and out of shape enough to be severely winded, but I imagined plenty of my countrymen and countrywomen would be courting heart attacks on those stairs. Old buildings, old towers, old monuments. No elevators.…. Potential infarctions lurk around every corner. That brief museum stop on the way up was a welcome break from the thigh-straining, lung-bursting climb and surely saved many of us from collapse.

At the top of the monument, Micki and I looked around, saw all twelve tree-lined avenues that converged on the spot (forming France's beloved star pattern), picked out the main sites we recognized, but mostly watched the crazy traffic below us. The Arc de Triomphe stands on an island in the middle of an enormous traffic circle. Supposedly, there are eight lanes in the circle, but I saw no lines indicating them. The twelve avenues that radiate out from it all dump their traffic in the same spinning congestion, trapping cars in the wrong lanes, resulting in a constant jockeying of position to somehow reach the outer layer and eventually exit the mess. My brother-in-law told me that, according to his Paris tour guide, insurance companies automatically split the cost of any accidents there rather than try to determine fault, because the chaotic traffic circle is an accident waiting to happen.

The first time I saw the Arc de Triomphe was with my grandmother, who was not energetic enough to attempt the

Endless spiral stairs in the Arc de Triomphe

climb. She wasn't even interested in taking the underground walkway to the island to view the monument from below, but was content to rest on a bench and watch the traffic in the circle as it performed its clumsy, elaborate dance, somehow avoiding constant collisions amid the din. It *was* fascinating, and we happily viewed and commented and were grateful that *we* didn't have to drive there as we waited for the rest of our group to make the climb and return. As absorbing as the traffic was at street level, it was even more compelling and entertaining from above, where Micki and I could really see the action.

While we were atop the arch, a couple of young French-speaking men approached Micki, holding their camera up in the international request for assistance. She responded in English, "If you want me to take your picture, I'll be glad to." The men happily switched to English, and we learned that they were Mormons, one of them from Mississippi. (Oh, how I would love to know how his French sounded to native speakers! Can the drawl be conquered?) They must have been newly arrived in the country if they couldn't immediately peg us as Americans. Still, I applaud them for addressing us in the language of the country we were in.

Micki took their picture, happy tourists at the moment, enjoying their visit to the Arc de Triomphe with the Eiffel Tower jutting up behind them. They made no attempt to tell us about their faith, for which we were grateful. But then, I've never found Mormons, even missionaries, to be pushy, as so many other door-to-door faith peddlers are. I knew a number of Mormons as fellow graduate students in the foreign language program we taught in at The University of Texas. They were uniformly decent, intelligent, diligent, and nice. Everyone was clean-cut, well-dressed, and physically attractive, too. Think Donny and Marie Osmond and you have the right picture. They, themselves—the salt-of-the-earth (Salt Lake-of-the-earth?) adherents—are Mormonism's best advertisement.

We took another lazy turn around the top of the monument, returning to the view down the broad, tree-lined Champs-Élysées. A young American couple stood next to us, also looking down "The Axe," the so-called axis of Paris: the straight line that runs from the Arc de Triomphe down the Champs-Élysées through the Place de la Concorde and Tuileries to the Louvre at the other end. The Place de la Concorde is Paris' largest square, formerly the Place de la Révolution and site of the "Black Widow" guillotine that separated so many heads from necks (including Marie Antoinette's and King Louis XVI's). In the center of the square stands an obelisk, and I'd like to think it's on the actual site of the guillotine. The ancient Egyptian obelisk is huge, more than 3,300 years old (although it didn't arrive in Paris until 1833), and covered with hieroglyphs. It punctuates the view down the avenue like an exclamation point at the end.

The woman standing next to us pointed down the avenue and asked her companion, "What's that stick?"

Stick?? I looked curiously, expecting to see a spindly stick somewhere. But, no. She was pointing to the foot of the Champs-Élysées, to the Place de la Concorde. Yes, from that distance, the obelisk was a bit small, but you could tell that up close it would tower impressively. It's an imposing 75-foot-tall, 280-ton granite monument, after all. A stick. Her companion didn't have a clue, either.

The next stop for us was the Trocadéro gardens, which are famous, as far as I can tell, mostly for being across the river from the Eiffel Tower and providing probably the best views of it. There are several museums located in the palace at the top of the gardens, but I've only been to the open terrace between the two wings of the building. The terrace provided not only a splendid view of the Eiffel Tower but a low wall to

Ancient Egyptian obelisk in the Place de la Concorde

sit on, late-afternoon shade, and a highly diverting collection of tourists, vendors, and street entertainers.

Happily seated and realizing that we were finally hungry again (hiking up monuments will do that to a body), we pulled out our slightly tattered apple tarts from lunch and ate them. They were delicious, though not as sweet as an American apple tart would be. The other tourists on the terrace did a fine job entertaining us, particularly a couple of thin young Japanese men. They were trying to position their camera low to the ground and time a picture just right to get one of them leaping through the air, apparently over the Eiffel Tower from that angle. This was clearly a difficult undertaking, as they attempted it again and again and again, until many of us watching were laughing with them as they doggedly tried— and failed—yet again. I imagine that many images showed the tower impaling a pair of pants (possibly in a sensitive location). I'm sure the jolly young men had a good laugh when they viewed the photos later.

We walked down the hill, past the fountains to the Eiffel Tower, fully aware that Tuesday tourist traffic was especially heavy here because the Louvre was closed on Tuesdays and more people ended up at the tower. But being so close, we went to look at it anyway. We dodged countless trinket salesmen on the way (five Eiffel Tower statuettes for one euro!) and walked across the bridge, where there were more street vendors selling more tower souvenirs. We then walked under the massive structure itself, which was also crowded with— you guessed it!—Eiffel Tower trinket salesmen.

As expected, the lines were far too long to mess with, so we decided to take a boat cruise that evening instead. Turning from the Eiffel Tower lines, we saw a shuttle parked at the curb to take people to Bateau Mouche (the boat tour we wanted), so we hopped on. It was interesting to drive along Paris in the traffic, even if we were on a little multi-car shuttle, hardly bigger than a string of golf carts. The only other time I had been in Paris traffic was when my grandmother and I splurged after visiting the Galeries Lafayette department store. We indulged in a taxi back to our hotel rather than endure a late-in-the-day public transportation odyssey. That ride, too, was extremely interesting, as our taxi driver unexpectedly zipped through the old arched drive at the Louvre and drove us right across the courtyard by the Tuileries before darting through the opposite wing of the Louvre to take us along the Seine. Then, as now on the way to our boat ride, it was especially nice not to have to walk any extra steps after tramping so many throughout the day, even with using the métro.

The Paris métro system is justifiably lauded for its range and ease of use. What is seldom mentioned, however, is that using it requires a great deal of walking and climbing. The underground passageways connecting the rail systems to the street level and to each other form their own subterranean network. Merely descending to the train platform can require walking through tunnels for ten minutes and, this being Europe, stairs for the depth changes are much more common than escalators, including stairs heading up. (That's right—there may not be an up-escalator!) The ample walking and climbing no doubt contribute to the general level of fitness of the typical Parisian. My grandmother found it difficult, at times, even though we took things slowly. Micki and I didn't take things slowly, and we gasped for breath on some of the climbs. I couldn't imagine trying to negotiate the many stairs or the train cars themselves with small children who might need to be carried or—God forbid—ride in a stroller. Perhaps the bus system is better suited for transporting the very young and the old and infirm.

By far more convenient than buses or the métro was the little shuttle we rode from the Eiffel Tower directly to the quay on the Seine. Conveniently dropped off near the boat ticket office, we bought our tickets and boarded very shortly before the next tour left. We sat on the open roof and, once underway, our tour boat became one of those that people on shore and bridges wave at, and the passengers wave in return. Everyone is so excited to be in Paris that they share their happiness with each other through those greetings.

We were surrounded by jabbering Japanese tourists, who apparently were not aware of what quiet travelers they are supposed to be. In fact, one middle-aged man near us was evidently quite a cutup, because he kept doing and saying things that sent the others into gales of laughter. We were just heading under the Pont Neuf, and I was reminding Micki about it being the oldest bridge in the city, despite its name of "new bridge," when, BOOM! Everyone lurched as the boat bumped against the support of the bridge. I amended my explanation to Micki to say that the Pont Neuf *used* to be the oldest bridge in Paris. (Ha! The Japanese comedian was rubbing off….) Fortunately, nothing and no one appeared to be harmed.

There *is* surprisingly little clearance under the bridges for boats, at least to my untrained eye. The graceful arches seem to skim just above the water level, and the boats ride so close to the underside of the bridges that it often seemed we could reach up and touch them. It must be more than my imagination that clearance is a little limited, because in 2002, on my trip with my grandmother and other family members, our boat ride was delayed until late in our stay because the river had been flowing too high from recent rains for the boats to run safely.

It started raining as we finished our ride, and Micki and I returned to our hotel, grateful that we had not waited in line to visit the Eiffel Tower in *that* weather. We had a quick grocery store stop, then twenty minutes of slow Internet use in the hotel lobby before we headed up to our room for supper. We wanted to call home next, but our phone card didn't work that night. Were we out of minutes already? It was hard to tell, because the lady on the recorded message only talked French to us, and not slowly enough for me to make any sense out of it.

Our hotel room, though small, was quite comfortable. We had a large bed that was really two twins shoved together. That is extremely common in European hotels, and I had always assumed it was for the versatility of placing the beds together for a roomy double or separating them for twins. I have moved households enough over the years, though (ten times in the last twenty-six years, to be exact), that I wonder whether households go with the smaller beds simply for maneuverability. After all, the challenges of hauling large, bulky beds up narrow, winding stairways and through hallways filled with jogs and choke points might not appeal to everyone. It's fairly common in old European city centers (especially on construction or renovation sites, but anyplace really, where heavy objects must be lifted up) to have small cranes protruding from the tops of buildings and a platform containing, say, bags of cement being hoisted up. Or a piano. Or other large furniture. Whatever the reason, the roomy double bed was not a problem for Micki and me, because we'd both grown up sharing a bed with a sister on occasion and, unlike the drivers around the Arc de Triomphe, we were good at keeping to our own "lanes."

Our room also had a large armoire with a small safe in it, but we didn't use either of them. We took our important things with us when we went out, and we lived out of our suitcases. As for valuable jewelry, forget it. We weren't traveling to impress people and certainly didn't want to mess with anything that might be stolen. I can't fathom traveling that way, to be honest. My travel jewelry generally consists of a pair of simple earrings or two and *possibly* a necklace that goes with almost everything I take along. Micki, of course, the queen of bling, brought much more, but nothing that would have been tragic to lose.

I had the left side of the room (and the bed); Micki had the right. We were glad to have a private bath, but, like most of the bathrooms we would encounter in France, it was small and awkward, having been carved out of a corner of the original room, which also rendered the bedroom smaller and less harmonious than it originally had been. The bathroom had a hairdryer, just a snaky tube that never really heated up. It had enough oomph to blow my long, loose dark hairs all over the white bathroom tiles, but that was about all it accomplished.

The shower was not roomy. The water temperature varied wildly during a single shower, depending on what other people in the building were doing. The shower head was adjustable up or down on a pole. Because the shower had been built into an existing room and the workers had to put the plumbing underneath it—or so I worked it out, anyway—the shower floor was six to eight inches above the floor of the bathroom, and every time I stepped out of it (half-blind without my glasses), I lunged to the floor, it was such a drop. Even though I knew it was coming, that first step was a tough one, and I hoped I wouldn't throw my hip out of whack—as I do on occasion—from the ungainly lurch when I landed. (I needed a trebuchet warning sign next to the shower!)

This second night was when I took action with my footwear. Micki and I had been wearing our trusty matching sandals, and the first evening in France, I noticed a funky odor coming from mine. Micki claimed that hers were getting stinky, too, but I thought she was just trying to make me feel better. (Later, at home, an Internet search quickly revealed that our brand of hiking sandals—as well as many others— was notorious for getting smelly. I felt strangely better about that, finding comfort in lots of company.) The smell was even worse by the end of day two in Paris, so, knowing that the sandals were washable, I soaped mine up in the shower and gave them a good cleaning. They were still a little damp the next day when we planned to visit the art museums, so I wore my backup, non-hiking sandals for the day. The result? A slight, though brief, improvement in odor, but I paid for it with two big blisters after wearing my alternate footwear.

But I get ahead of myself. First, another welcome trip to bed.

5
Ugly Americans

Wednesday brought us another glorious summer day, and we had a lot on our schedule. After sleeping late, we left the hotel at nine, buying *pain au chocolat* (flaky rolls filled with chocolate) at our local bakery for breakfast. We then mailed our postcards and went into the local post office to buy a new phone card. This postal lady was also extremely nice and helpful, not at all as I'd read that the post office personnel are. Had I been misled, or was this part of an August vacation craziness, where everything was turned on its head?

We descended to the métro to ride to the Place de la Concorde, and this time Micki's card wouldn't go through the machine. At this point, I was still on my fifth card and she was on her third. I had purposely left my sunglass clip in the room, so I wouldn't have that magnet anywhere near where I kept my transit card. I am happy and relieved to report that my card still worked at the end of the day.

Once we had two working transit passes, we headed to the Orangerie, now an art museum. There we admired a variety of Impressionist paintings, including Monet's huge water lily series. The water lily scenes merited some serious gawking, the way the splotchy, messy, thick layering of paint somehow softened and coalesced into a soothing, harmonious whole from a distance.

We crossed the river for a three-hour visit to the Musée d'Orsay for more Impressionists—Monet, Manet, Renoir, Degas, Mary Cassatt. I was pleased to see a woman painter exhibited among all the men, and an American, at that. The museum was packed with tourists, and the upper floors of the building were undergoing renovations of some sort. Because of that, many of the paintings were relocated to halls on the first floor, which further limited any space to view in peace.

With two museums behind us by midday, Micki and I crossed the Seine again for another "Pauls" cart lunch outside the Louvre—in the shade again, because I was quite sunburnt from the previous day's sightseeing. We slipped into the Louvre via the Museum Pass door (no wait!) and spent four hours there, lost the whole time. Eventually, we did stumble across the Mona Lisa—small and distant because of the crowd, just a sea of heads between us and the painting. We passed the Venus de Milo and Winged Victory statues many times, as we kept circling around looking for other things. We recognized some of the paintings we kept looping by; mostly, though, we didn't know the works, and we spent as much time admiring the former palace as we did the artwork.

After a while, we left the packed "must-see" Denon wing and ventured into the other two wings of the museum, which were refreshingly less crowded. We happily wandered past giant Mesopotamian friezes and eventually found our way to Napoleon III's apartments. Despite greatly reduced crowds in those areas of the museum, it was still very warm, and we sighed in relief each time we walked over an air-conditioning grate in the floor, as we were both wearing skirts that caught the cool breeze. No Marilyn Monroe peepshow resulted,

Modern glass pyramid in the Louvre courtyard

though. These were modest, calf-length skirts that did no more than bell out a bit.

We left the Louvre about seven and went to the Eiffel Tower, where the line wasn't as ridiculously long as it had been the previous day, but it was still plenty lengthy. It slowly wove its way back and forth through the cattle chutes we were lined up in, and as we zigzagged through, we became familiar with our fellow tourists by sight and sound. And they were, by and large, not a sophisticated group, but rather boisterous, having a good time on vacation, except possibly those families with sullen or bickering children. The variety of languages mixed and clashed, with none dominating, not even English or French. What a pleasure it was to be in such an international mix, where any groups even approaching ignorant or obnoxious behavior were not Americans. (See? It's not just us!)

While most groups wore informal clothing, even track

suits, the couple in front of us seemed positively French, they were so chicly dressed and soft-spoken. The woman wore a blindingly white jumpsuit, which was just about the last thing I would choose to travel in. Every spill would show, and you'd have to strip half-naked to pee. The man was wearing black slacks and a white sports coat, and the couple looked good. After at least half an hour shuffling alongside each other, we struck up a conversation and discovered that they were English teachers from the country of Georgia. Not surprisingly, their English was superb. I didn't even know for sure what they speak in Georgia, I confessed when Micki asked me that later, although I guessed Russian. (Wrong! The majority speak a separate Georgian language, I learned at home.)

My previous Eiffel Tower visit was quite a different story. Emily and I had to wait for *ages* in line, directly behind two other American couples, who didn't know each other at all at the start of our wait but very likely knew each other quite well enough by the end of it. One couple was modestly dressed in dark colors and conversed quietly between themselves, nicely in keeping with French expectations and practice. The other couple, however—bright colors, bold patterns, loud voices— soon engaged them in a conversation from which there was no escape, for them as well as the many of us in the zigzagging line around them.

The loud woman could have been the model for "An Ugly American in Paris." The woman was in no way physically ugly, but she was either completely clueless about the social habits of French people or she didn't care at all that she stood out like a sore thumb, which is where the "ugly" label comes from. These people unintentionally give Americans a bad name abroad, because they so heedlessly—and so needlessly—violate local practices and expectations. This woman unconsciously broke so many French social rules that she made herself look bad—ill-mannered, gauche, rude. She wore heavy make-up.

She spoke very loudly (and constantly). She wore bright patterns and showy jewelry. She complained (loudly) about the wait and about her hotel room. She shared how much she had paid for her hotel, for her purse, for her dinner. None of these points would stand out on a tourist in the United States, but in France, she looked like an obnoxious American. I saw others regarding her with disapproval, and I spoke softly in German to Emily, trying to disguise my nationality.

Another group of Americans was farther ahead in the line, a group of nicely dressed black men. We occasionally passed them, and from snatches of their conversations that we heard, it was clear that they were musicians, and they were taking a break from recording an album. The obvious leader of their trio was the tallest and wore a long black leather coat, a black cap, and had a black-and-white keyboard-patterned scarf tucked into the neckline of his coat. He looked like someone I should know, but I couldn't place him. When we were situated such that I could snap a picture for later identification, I pretended to focus on the tower, but made sure to include him in the shot.

Unfortunately, he was on to me and covered his face with his hand to block my view. I felt bad about making him feel pursued and resolutely ignored him for the rest of our visit, including when we ended up riding the same elevator to the top with him, when we were on the top observation deck with him, and when I rounded a corner and we just about collided. Still, it kills me to this day not to know who we were with. Who is so famous that he suspects paparazzi and shields his face from a small camera across a crowd? He was too young to be Quincy Jones, I think. Was it a Marsalis brother? Who else plays keyboard and produces recordings in France? I'm not familiar enough with the music scene to know, and the partial-face photo I have of the man has not been very helpful.

After a forty-five minute wait, Micki and I were able to ride the elevators up the tower, but only to the second level. By the time we reached the ticket booth, they were not allowing people to the third (the highest) level, although we didn't know why not. While the second level is said to have the best views, Micki was disappointed, because she had wanted to go all the way to the top. Clearly, we need to return to Paris so she can do this. By the time we came down from the tower, the pulsing evening lightshow had begun on it, which was rather hard to appreciate standing right in the midst of it. We left quickly to try to view it from the gardens below, but caught very little of the display. At 10:15, we walked (or limped, in my case, because of my fresh blisters) the length of the Champ de Mars (the park that stretches beyond the tower), and we visited our grocery store for drinks and fruit. Then back to our home away from home.

Despite the idiosyncrasies of our lodging—the chopped-up room, the raised shower floor, the temperamental hot water, the slow Internet—our hotel was a nice one, in a sedate residential area of Paris. As Micki and I had never traveled together before, and her other trips I'd heard about sounded fairly luxurious, I went with an established location and the American standards of a TV and—very welcome in August— air conditioning. That seemed like such an American excess in energy-conscious Europe, with its sky-high electrical costs and general lack of air conditioning, but, heavens, it was nice! Our hotel was one recommended by travel writer and TV host Rick Steves—and I've even seen it show up in his Paris shows—so I suspect they get a lot of American tourists.

I also suspect that many Americans want their rooms COLD. Apparently, the staff thought that if we were paying for AC, we should get the full benefit of it. When we entered the room for the first time, it was blessedly cool, but we knew we would be gone for a while, so we turned it down. Every day we turned it down (well, actually, turned the temperature up), and every day the housekeeping staff made it chilly again. That seemed a great waste of electricity (particularly when we were gone all day) for a country that likes to conserve energy.

Our second day in Paris, it was downright cold in the room. Micki turned the air down before bed, but we still froze, particularly me, I think because I went to bed with wet hair (having just taken my shower and lurched half-blind to the floor for the night). The next morning, talking about how cold it had been, Micki realized that she had turned the *temperature* lower before bed, rather than turning the intensity of the AC down. No wonder the socks I had pulled on weren't enough to keep me warm through the night.

We wouldn't make the same mistake this next night. After eating, writing, and showering, we adjusted the temperature properly and lay our tired bodies down to recuperate for the next day's adventures.

6
Stay Off the Grass!

You can't turn around in Paris without bumping into history—glorious, brutal, passion-filled. Its ghosts, good and bad, are everywhere. Every old building has a story to tell, every town square a checkered past. I didn't assign Micki the same amount of homework I did young Emily before we traveled, but I did press her to read a couple of the same short biographies. One of them was about Napoleon, former general and emperor, and his tumultuous, victorious, ultimately tragic life.

Our hotel was close to Napoleon's tomb, and throughout our days in Paris, we could see the towering golden dome of the building glinting in the sun. Finally, after another nice sleep-in on our fourth day in Paris, we were ready to venture around the corner and pay our respects. We ate some fruit and walked the short distance to the Hôtel des Invalides, the former refuge for wounded veterans, and worked our way around the back of the complex to the Dôme Church, where Napoleon's body lies.

August favored us with another beautiful, sunny day. The

formal gardens on the grounds boasted a tidy profusion of flowers and shrubs that drank in the sunlight. We admired some of the flower beds from the path and then turned to take pictures of the approach to the church. Positioning myself to get as much of the building as I could in my viewfinder, I eyed the rope fence bordering the grass and, keeping well away from it, I lifted one foot off the gravel path and partially placed it on the half-bare, half-brown edge of "lawn," safely distant from the rope fence.

TWEEEEEEEEEE!!!!! A harsh whistle shrilled, and not the admiring kind. Two police officers standing guard near the street had seen my toes encroach on the dry grass, and that was not to be tolerated. They gestured for me to step back. Alarmed, I sprang back onto the path, abashed to be officially scolded for such a small infraction, when I was nowhere near the roped-off area. There was a sign nearby, a "Prohibited Lawn" sign showing a crossed-off shoe print, but I really thought that was to keep us from cutting *across* the lawn, actually walking on it, past where the rope fence was. But, no, clearly *no contact whatsoever* was allowed with the dead remnants of grass.

I had read about the French obsession with keeping off the grass, remembering particularly the wry comments in one of my all-time favorite books, *Spend it Foolishly*. In the novel, a young American woman ends up working as an unhappy *au pair* in dreary winter Paris before escaping to sunny Italy. She laments that with all the beautiful parks in Paris, no one is allowed on the grass, so I was prepared for strict rules.

I had actually been surprised on the first day of our visit, when Micki and I had briefly visited the Luxembourg Gardens in the Latin Quarter. I had long heard of the famous Luxembourg Gardens and had even stayed within easy walking distance of them once, but I was with my elderly grandmother at the time, and the distance would have tired her out too

Stay off the lawn. They mean it!

much, so we never visited. I made sure to swing by on this trip, however, because Micki loves flowers and plants. The gardens were certainly attractive—elaborate flower beds laid out between gravel paths and circling around statues, with expanses of green lawn between them. The surprising part of our visit was that we saw people sitting and lying on the grass. *On the grass! In the park!* I had thought that there was a blanket prohibition against doing that, but here were parents and children, young lovers, all lolling about on the greenery. Perhaps the rules were relaxed in August.

Micki and I watched the families enjoying the sunshine. We took pictures of burgeoning flower beds, of flower-ringed statues, and managed not to climb into any of the displays to get good shots of each other, as some Japanese girls did. They were lucky no security guards saw *them*, or they might have been hauled in for questioning. Or maybe simply expelled from the country.

Of course, staying off the grass is not the only thing the

French are famously picky about. You're supposed to keep to yourself, keep quiet, and respect the privacy of others, as I had read a great deal about before ever traveling to France. I am also acutely aware that we Americans—a fairly boisterous people—are naturally at odds with that philosophy, and we're not about to let the expectations of another country stifle our vocalizations.

As such, I may have gone a bit overboard in shushing others and reminding them to be quiet. At any rate, on an earlier trip it slipped out that my nephew, walking down Boulevard Saint-Germain in Paris with my sister and the rest of their family, had sneezed in public (presumably loudly), whereupon the others told him not to let me hear that or I would lecture him about being quiet. (Or something along those lines.) It's true—I probably would have cringed at a violent nasal explosion. Surely a French person would have been more discreet and produced only the smallest of little *choos*, barely audible. I just hope the others told my nephew *in an undertone* how I would have reacted, and I'm confident the French are with me on this.

The leniency at the Luxembourg Gardens had not prepared me for the strict enforcement before the church that held Napoleon's tomb. I think Micki has a picture of me airborne after the shock of the whistle, but as she is unbelievably slow about getting her pictures printed or in any sort of order, I don't know that for sure, because I haven't seen them. This is a definite drawback of Micki's artistic bent. Three years after our trip, she finally started scrapbooking her photos and memorabilia. She had maybe twelve pages done, and then didn't touch the project again for months. (For years?) As for me, it may take me a few weeks (or even months—I wait for a good sale) to get my pictures printed, but then I slap them into a photo album or two and am done. I can look at them or show them to others whenever I like. I have to admit, though, that if she continues as she has started, Micki will have a stunning account of our trip to share with the six or so of our family and friends who haven't died of old age by then.

I know I took a picture of the two policemen, with their flat-topped pillbox hats and their pants tucked into military boots. They were both buff and handsome young men, very self-important, which I guess you are allowed to be if you have the authority to whistle rebukes at menacing middle-aged Sunday School teachers. The one with muscular crossed arms in short sleeves was wearing sunglasses and looking straight at me, coldly intimidating. Obviously, I was up to no good, and he needed to keep an eye on me. Who knew where the

Police officers at Napoleon's Tomb

destruction would end otherwise? Maybe I would hitch up my A-line skirt and rampage across the actual *grass*, and where would public safety be then?

Getting past the embarrassment of being publicly chastised (barely), I found the church and the tomb both impressive and beautiful. We entered the building through towering gilded doors, perhaps twelve feet high. The massive tomb lies in the crypt on the floor of a soaring rotunda, directly below the heavenly painted dome high above. We leaned over the circular white marble rail and admired it from the main level before descending to view it up close. Napoleon rests inside six coffins, and his deep red sarcophagus stands on a giant green granite pedestal, creating a hulking memorial for a legendarily diminutive man. (Legend appears to be off on this. Napoleon seems to have been of average height for his day, something around five feet, six inches.) I loved all the inlaid stonework in the floor, marble and granite and I don't know what all, forming a giant laurel wreath and sunburst around the tomb and, elsewhere, a lovely Napoleon medallion with an emperor's crown.

All impressive and lovely, but we had much to see for the day, so off we walked around the corner to the Rodin museum, located in the sculptor's former house and gardens. A line stretched outside the entrance, and we had to wait several minutes on the sidewalk before we could enter. Across the street were two police vans and, although there was no appearance of alarm or hurry, the men were dressing in seriously protective gear: bullet-proof vests, shin and knee guards, armored plates over the shoulders and upper arms. These guys, with their closely shaved heads, looked to be a different breed from the officers who had just tootled at me with their whistle. (Although even the whistlers had worn sidearms, so clearly France does not mess around on the policing front.)

I never saw what the three or four riot officers ended

Napoleon's tomb

up doing (perhaps they were sent to arrest tourists who actually stepped *into* the flower beds) because we had reached the Rodin ticket area and were distracted by the businesslike security check before we entered the museum proper. I had been to the Rodin museum when I'd had Emily with me, and the welcome had felt completely different. In late winter then, there were comparatively few tourists. There was no sign of any riot police. The security officers at the entrance talked with Emily, playfully teasing her, asking her whether she was enjoying Paris and complimenting her on her passport photo. She smiled broadly and assured them that she was having a wonderful time.

That wasn't the only time little Emily was spoken to in a playful manner by Frenchmen, which was quite delightful. We were also addressed by a Frenchman on the RER train to Versailles. He was on his way to golf in the suburbs, and he talked to Emily (and then me) as we sat across from each other on the trip. There was another Frenchman on the shuttle bus at Disney Paris at the end of a long day at the Magic Kingdom. His worn-out child was next to him, and my child was next to me. I guess that I initiated that conversation, commenting that his boy was *fatigué* (tired), and somehow, despite the language barrier, we shared some parental sympathy about how exhausting the Disney experience was.

I don't know whether it's significant that all our spontaneous communications were with men; they were not remotely flirtatious. Yet, my only exchanges with women were to ask for directions, and I carefully looked out for older ladies to approach, reasoning, probably falsely, that they would be more likely to want to be helpful. I can recall only one Frenchwoman who ever spoke to me. She was a beautifully dressed middle-aged woman at the next table when my grandmother and I sat at the window of a café, drinking *kir* cocktails and watching the throng of humanity stream by outside. I had noticed the sophisticated woman sitting next to us, with her tangerine sweater, a matching scarf flung artfully around her shoulders, slowly inhaling on her cigarette while she read her paperback. She addressed me at some point to ask me to look out for her things while she went to the restroom. We were only too happy to do so, of course, friendly Iowans called into action. And that was it, other than a quick *merci* when she returned. It didn't help that on my various trips I could speak only the most basic idiot French, and my companions none at all. Why, oh why, could no one ask us a question in German?

I simultaneously long to know French and curse it for being so difficult. How do you learn a language where half the letters of a word or phrase aren't even pronounced? Or if they are pronounced, it's in a completely foreign way? Where *Louvre* is pronounced "loov" and *sept* is "set" and *huit* is "weet" and *trois* is "trwah"? (I remember sharing a flight with French people and hearing their pronunciation of our destination: "day-trwah" for Detroit.) What learner can look at *Est-ce que vous avez....?* ("Do you have ...?") and figure out it's spoken "es-kuh voo zah-vay"? In what kind of language is the word for lawyer pronounced the same as the word for avocado? "Pork" the same as "port"? In an impossible language, that's what.

What do you do with a language like this, one that names its numbers in a perfectly orderly fashion (*if* hard to spell and pronounce), until it reaches the seventies, at which point it gleefully starts with its teens again, having apparently lost its word for "seventy"? Instead, in French you get sixty-ten, sixty-eleven, sixty-twelve, etc., all the way up to eighty, which is where the joke intensifies. They don't have "eighty" in French; they have "four-twenties." And then, to really put the icing on the crazy cake, "ninety" is "four-twenties-ten." You get to go like that all the way through the teens again before reaching one hundred. My creaky, rusted brain does not easily come up with "four-twenties-thirteen" if I want to say, for example, ninety-three. As a rank beginner, I have to remember that I need four-twenties for the base form, remember that I need to add thirteen to that, and then desperately search my mental files for the French equivalents of those.

It seems such a difficult, illogical language, utterly unattainable for us mere mortals who think pronunciation should have at least a passing acquaintance with spelling. Consequently, even if I could have found French people who would talk with me, any social interaction was fatally handicapped by my lack of French language skills.

Those brief exchanges with Emily were just about the only times I was able to interact with actual French people who weren't service personnel. Micki and I were not even that fortunate; with no child to act as a gateway, we were not able to breach French reserve and connect at all. Not that we were actively trying to speak with locals, but she and I are both friendly, outgoing, talkative individuals, and the only people we'd managed to chat with on our visit so far were the American Mormons on the Arc de Triomphe and the English teachers from Georgia at the Eiffel Tower. We would have enjoyed getting to know some French people, even just a little bit. Instead, I felt like Kerry, the American *au pair* in *Spend it Foolishly*, longing to embrace the beautiful city of Paris, to belong in it in some small sense, but repeatedly being rebuffed. I was free to visit, but I was not part of it. How could I be, when no one would talk to me?

Certainly, the security guards at the Rodin Museum weren't chatting us up. They were all business. But so were we, at that point. Once we were through the checkpoint, we went into the house first, where it soon became apparent that Rodin was a dirty old man. He had many nude sculptures, of course, which was to be expected, but also a big statue of female genitalia, and what about all those mistresses he bedded over the years? (Helpfully revealed courtesy of the artwork explanations.) He must have been a big fan of the author Balzac, as there were multiple sculptures of him, including a large bronze nude, and—believe me—with his beach-ball stomach, Balzac did not have the figure for it.

The walled gardens surrounding the house exuded peace and beauty. They stretched away from the back of the house about as far as a football field, it seemed. What an ideal place for a home, I thought, in a little mansion in a private garden in the heart of Paris. Improbable fantasies kicked in. Could I win a boatload of money and live in Rodin's house at least part-time? I would take care of the place. I would even allow the Balzac sculpture to stay. (Although the giant genitalia would *have* to go in the basement.) If the property belonged to me, I would be able to tread carefully across the grass in back. Just a little bit on a beautiful summer day. And that urge on its own, I realized sadly, disqualified me from living there, from living in Paris at all.

Rodin bronze of the writer Balzac

Rodin's garden on his walled Paris estate

We completed our wander through the gardens, imagining long-ago ladies in their long gowns who had done the same, but, unlike us, who were possibly meeting their lovers in the shrubbery for trysts. (Very likely they were meeting randy Rodin himself, from what we'd read.) So quiet and evocative were the shaded paths, I could easily see old figures drifting along them. There were more statues in the gardens, both back and front, including The Thinker, whom we visited before leaving the estate.

With lunchtime upon us, I remembered a gyro stand in the Latin Quarter that my grandmother and I had frequented a couple of times when we were in Paris. It was just a short métro ride away, so Micki and I headed there next. We located the food stand easily enough and both ordered a gyro and fries. As I stood at the service window and received my heavily freighted, flimsy cardboard lunch basket, a pigeon lit on the sign above the window and relieved itself, its droppings just missing my lunch—by no more than an inch or two—as they fell to the ground. Supposedly, French people think it's good luck to step in dog poop. I wondered fleetingly whether the luck extended to being hit by pigeon poop. If I hadn't already disliked pigeons as dirty, pushy birds, having one ruin my lunch would have taken care of that. As it was, the close call merely intensified my aversion.

We carried our food across the river to the square in front of Notre-Dame, where we sat on low walls and ate the best we could among the aggressive pigeons. They relentlessly encroached on our space, crowding our feet and hovering near us, looking for handouts. It was so bad that Micki actually backhanded a couple that were flying into our faces. What is it about that square and birds? My grandmother and I were fascinated by a man we saw there who was happily covered with sparrows as he fed them. Yech. That's the problem, of course; people feed them. Micki and I battled the pigeons our whole meal, and when we were finished, threw our remaining bread away rather than encourage the nasty gray marauders. It was our fourth day in Paris, and we had not bought any souvenirs yet, so we tramped back to the Left Bank for some serious trinket shopping. The shops on the quaintly medieval rue de la Huchette burst with economical items for the frugal or budget-challenged tourist. Here we were able to buy all the scarves and ties and other knickknacks we wanted for our loved ones at home, as well as a few for ourselves.

I looked at berets for my little blues-playing son but didn't see anything that was particularly good. I did see a Paris version of a Rubik's cube—a recent enthusiasm of his—which I immediately snatched up for him. Little did I realize that he wouldn't be able to solve the cube because of its very Frenchness. The six sides showed six different scenes from Paris. Fine and dandy, in its completed state, and a fine reminder of the City of Light. Once scrambled, however, with the sides all twisted around, the cube was virtually impossible to solve. Each piece of each of the six similarly colored Paris pictures had to not only be on the right *face* of the cube, but also be located in the correct one of nine *positions* on that face and with the right *orientation*, so all the pieces of the pictures fit together and had the same version of "up." And, unlike the original cube with its bright primary colors, there was no way to quickly identify which groups of squares were even supposed to go together. I can look at a red square and see that it goes on the side with the other red squares, but a square with part of a sunset and a piece of some dark structure?? Not a clue. My apologies to my son, who gave it a good twist or two before we realized the danger of doing so. The cube stood half-scrambled on a shelf in his bedroom for ages, a worthy reminder of my confusion in France.

My daughter fared much better. She is easy to buy for and got a scarf of the pashmina sort that you can now find in department stores all across America. Poor John got another tie, this time of Monet's water lilies. It can join his Eiffel Tower tie and the *fleur de lis* tie I brought him from earlier trips.

Since we were in the neighborhood, Micki and I went to the Cluny museum, where we examined the Lady with the Unicorn tapestries—medieval sex symbols, if you believe the descriptions we read. (I suppose the unicorn does look pretty pleased when the lady caresses his horn.) We also viewed the old Roman baths and rooms of Middle Age artifacts before succumbing to the pull of more trinkets, this time on the sedate rue Cler. I got two t-shirts for the kids (and promptly lost my receipt), and Micki got a sweatshirt. Yes, we were true Americans when it came to shopping. Give us a deal on some low-class clothing plastered with the name of the place we were visiting, and we were happy.

Now our shopping blood was really up, and we returned to the Champs-Élysées to the Swarovski store, where Micki bought her necklace and earrings, and I bought the green charm I'd looked at for Emily. I salivated over a lot of other shiny baubles but knew I was unlikely to wear them, however much I admired them, so I saved my money and vowed to bring home experiences and photographs, not mounds of trinkets. If nothing else, I should be able to get a fabulous print of me jumping into the air in alarm at Napoleon's Tomb. I should frame it along with my photo of the two officers looking coldly intimidating. Stay off the grass, indeed.

Now *that* would be an apt reminder of Paris.

7
French Twist

Cheap, trashy, touristy—that's how many see the Latin Quarter these days (and maybe always have), but I have a certain fondness for it. Maybe it's because students and immigrants congregate there, making it, on the one hand, one of the more vibrant sections of Paris, and, on the other, relatively affordable compared to the many swish districts in that posh city. In any case, when it was time to do large-scale souvenir shopping, we headed to the Latin Quarter, and it didn't disappoint. Same with the cheap eats. I was sad to observe that the area was noticeably dirty and littered when Micki and I were there, in a way I did not recall from when I had stayed there before with my grandmother, on my first trip to France.

I had been the unofficial travel agent for that earlier trip, scouting locations not just for the two of us, but for my sister and her family, who would need a room for four to house them. Thank God for online searches, where I was able to quickly rule out most Paris hotels right off the bat. (Old buildings. Small rooms. Few quads.) Further limited by considering only affordable hotels, and centrally-located ones, and, ideally, those with breakfast included, we soon ended up in the Latin Quarter, just minutes from Notre-Dame Cathedral and even closer to several easy métro stops. The Sorbonne was only a couple of blocks away.

The hotel did not have an elevator, as so many don't, so I made sure to tell the manager in advance that I would be there with my elderly grandmother, who really was not in terrific shape, but probably not as decrepit as I made her sound. I suffered a pang or two of guilt later when we saw our fellow hotel guest, a shrunken and bent old woman in Indian-looking clothes, shuffling up and down the many stairs to her room on deformed and swollen feet. Nonetheless, I was well aware that climbing stairs multiple times a day would be an ordeal for my grandmother, so I was grateful to find that we had been placed in the one bedroom on ground level.

This was the hotel owned and run by Paul, the Frenchman who had nothing whatsoever to do with the Paul I would deliver to the world about nine months later. Sure, our room location just across a small hall from the reception desk would certainly allow my husband to speculate, should he choose to, and should he conveniently ignore the fact that I was with my grandmother the whole time and never exchanged more than a *bonjour* with the innkeeper. And if that weren't enough, I had my brother-in-law chaperoning me, as became clear later in the week.

We loved the location of the hotel (although a couple of years later it would be near ground zero of some violent student protests), but it was a funky cross between a hotel and a youth hostel. Our room was spartan, with a double bed, a twin bed, an armoire, a bedside table, and one straight-backed chair. There were no decorations. No TV. No phone. We had a private bathroom that was immaculate.

The quad that my sister's family occupied was several levels up, on the third floor, I think (which really means the fourth floor, to us non-Europeans). Their room was tight, with extra beds stuffed into it. When the bathroom was added to the room, it was done strangely, so that the bathroom walls extended only up to the decorative molding around the top of the wall, not all the way to the ceiling.

Paul, the hotel guy, talked to my brother-in-law about that at the reception desk one day, asking whether the room was all right. He explained that he could rent that one only to Americans, because Europeans, Asians, and Middle Easterners couldn't handle the bathroom not being completely private. Europeans were uncomfortable with the ceiling gap? How very odd. Generally, it's Europeans who are far earthier about their bodies and about bodily functions than most Americans are. Of course, the typical European public toilet has stall walls that extend floor to ceiling, giving a completely private cubicle, so maybe Americans are the earthy ones when it comes to bathrooms.

We were served breakfast each day in this hotel, a continental fare of hot drink, orange juice, a partial baguette, butter, jam, and fruit cocktail. We also had full access to a compact ground-floor kitchen, where French families sometimes prepared their evening meals. The breakfast room also served as a gathering place or lounge, and our group frequently met up there to make plans, compare experiences, and eat our takeout or grocery-store suppers together.

A highlight of the breakfast room was the large row of windows that looked out to the street. We could watch the traffic and pedestrians, observe the students climbing the spiral staircase to enter the building across the street (I think it was an architectural school), and watch other tourists loaded with luggage bump their way down the sidewalk, looking down to consult their instructions and then looking up for building numbers. By far the most fun, though, was the time a parking spot opened up right before the large central window, providing ongoing entertainment during that particular breakfast room visit.

The car that had left must have been wedged into the spot, or else it was one of those tiny Smart micro-cars, because the open parking space was far too small to accommodate even a compact vehicle. But that didn't stop people from trying! Driver after driver screeched to a halt when they saw the opening, backed in, tried to swing the front in, to no avail. Some drivers realized after one attempt that basic geometry would not allow their car to fit, but others were more determined. They would twist around in their seats, spin their steering wheels this way and that, but all for naught. Even with the accepted French practice of actually nudging the cars both fore and aft, they could not make their cars fit. Eventually, all roared off, with those who had tried the longest being the most visibly disgusted. No one succeeded on our watch. It was most amusing.

A similar incident occurred when my grandmother and I were on the rue Saint Jacques near Notre-Dame. A compact parking spot opened up on the street, wantonly broadcasting its siren call to those driving by. Almost the first passing vehicle could not resist—a hulking red Chevy Suburban. My grandmother and I were on the sidewalk watching, and all the patrons in the window of the café behind us also turned to view the show, seeming to lean forward in eager anticipation. The driver backed into the spot, leaving enough vehicle in the street at the front end to create at least a Smart car. Even a deluded Parisian driver could see that that was never going to work, so the Suburban soon continued down the street, ending a brief but highly entertaining diversion. (Who in their right mind drives a Suburban in Paris? Where would that behemoth be able to park in the city? On a landing strip?)

I think I'm drawn to those never-going-to-work parking attempts because I absolutely hate parallel parking, and I'm not very good at it. I'll get into the parking space eventually, but what should be a simple "back in, turn the nose in, done" sort of action ends up being a prolonged shuffle of backward, crank the wheel, forward, crank the wheel, backward, crank the wheel, etc., gradually edging the car to the curbside in an easy nine or ten motions. Somewhere in there I usually get at least one tire wedged up so tightly against the curb that I can't budge in one direction and have to backtrack before I can advance any farther. A champion car parker I am not. Therefore, it amuses me greatly to see people attempt parking feats that even I could immediately see were impossible. I especially enjoyed knowing that I was a foot traveler for the week and would never have to squeeze a car in anywhere in Paris.

I had actually read about parking problems in Paris before we embarked on that first trip, along with the need for pedestrians to be on guard for drivers who would not respect crosswalks (which would be most of them). Much of my preparation, though, focused on learning about the countless social differences between Americans and French people. Different ways of eating, greeting, shopping, and interacting in general.

One of the differences that had impressed me most deeply was what American expatriate Polly Platt (author of *French or Foe*) called The Look, a sexually charged, sweeping head-to-toe visual caress that is supposed to be a compliment to the woman receiving it. Coming from a fairly Puritan background (literally—the family genealogist says we descend from an indentured servant on the Mayflower, one George Soule), it all sounded too intense for my taste, but given my down-to-earth, completely Plain Jane looks, there was little chance I would have to deal with it.

I had shared this French cultural information with my relatives before we left, and my grandmother and I, at least, were curious to see whether we would see any evidence of the fabled French sexuality, any instances of The Look.

One morning, as we readied ourselves for the day, I rolled my hair up into a French twist and secured it with a large, curved, claw-like comb. This is a style that looks achingly glamorous on Audrey Hepburn when she is in Paris with Cary Grant in the movie *Charade*, but considerably less so on me. Sturdy, I could be called. Practical. But never glamorous. I well knew I could never be mistaken for a Frenchwoman by the way I dressed, moved, or acted, but I could at least go with an authentic hairstyle.

"You know, you can really see the gray at the sides when you wear your hair like that," my sister informed me in that helpful way siblings have. I didn't care. I didn't have that much gray. My hair was out of the way, it was relatively neat looking, and, in my head, at least, the style lent me a wisp—a bare hint—of sophistication. We left the building to venture forth for the day.

My grandmother and I turned to the right outside the hotel, heading to the nearest métro stop. We chatted happily with each other, and when we met a Frenchman on the sidewalk, I saw him staring at me intently. Quickly, I dropped my eyes.

"Did you see that?!" my grandmother whispered urgently after he had passed. "That man gave you The Look!"

I blushed and thought, indeed, as Polly Platt had written, there was no mistaking the penetrating Look when it was directed at a person. I guess it just went to show that, as Platt noted, you didn't have to be young or gorgeous to merit a Look. Or, as we might put it where I'm from, it takes all kinds. It was the kind of look that would easily be considered rude back home—far too intrusive—but here I was supposed to consider it a compliment. It just flustered and bewildered me.

So many things in France were backwards from what we were used to. Social rules are all twisted, turned around from those in the United States and most other Western countries. White is black in France, and black is white. Don't smile unless there's a good reason to. Don't make eye contact. Don't say hello to people on the street. Don't invade their space at all, physically, visually, audibly. Don't chat with strangers. Don't talk about work, family, health, money. Don't mix social levels. Don't flaunt wealth or wear flashy items or brag. Do be cold and reserved. Do be rude and snub people if they're not following the rules—that's part of being well-mannered in France.

The rules were as confusing and scrambled as the crazy, mixed-up picture pieces on my son's Rubik's cube—upside down, sideways, on the wrong side of my "social experience" cube altogether. Sure, it all made sense and snapped into place if you knew what you were doing, what was going on, but we didn't. We were Americans. Friendly, chatty, loud Americans. Worse yet, we were from Iowa, where it is bred into us to greet all we meet with a smile and a hello. Most of us love to talk with strangers. We happily discuss prices. I will say that we didn't flaunt wealth in Paris, but that could be because we didn't *have* wealth, not enough to flaunt, anyway. So, yes, I knew about French reserve and privacy, I knew that eye contact and smiles should be avoided with people I didn't know (which was everyone in the country). It was just so hard not to react naturally!

My pre-trip reading had also informed me that love affairs were common in France, for men and women. Discreet affairs are routine and accepted. Sex is not a big deal or a dirty deed—it's just part of life. I remember reading about a respectable French businesswoman who wrote a book detailing her sexual encounters, often with anonymous strangers in public places, dozens of lovers, known and unknown. While (as I recall, at least) even the French were said to be taken aback by the number of casual partners this woman had

had, she was not made a pariah. Sex, even extramarital sex or voluminous casual sex, is just another of life's physical appetites. This casual attitude toward sex and fidelity certainly contradicted my own practices and beliefs. My morals were in conflict with French codes, a clanging, deafening dissonance, but fortunately the clash was purely abstract, at least at this point, and I could ignore it.

Later in our stay, after our sidewalk encounter with The Look, my grandmother and I went to a small supermarket on our way back to our hotel in the evening. After selecting our food and wine, we waited in a long line that stretched back into the last aisle of the store. Speaking quietly with her about the frozen seafood displayed next to us (tiny frozen octopi were visible in a clear bag), I realized that the man in line ahead of us was watching me intently, and we had eye contact (deep, searing, very personal) before I quickly looked away, blushing, I'm sure. That should have been the end of it. But in my discomfort, I occasionally slid a glance in his direction, just to see whether he was still watching. He was, as piercingly as before, his dark eyes locked on mine. My face warmed even more.

As our checkout line advanced past the narrow aisle that had been confining us, it split into two lines for two cashiers. The man went left. I, a practical American, realized that the left line was much shorter than the right, so I also went that way. I continued to talk quietly with my grandmother, studiously ignoring the Frenchman now. Soon he checked out and, to my relief, he left the store. My grandmother and I soon left, as well.

When we exited the building, though, there was the man, standing outside. As we walked down the sidewalk the few blocks to our hotel, the man shadowed us across the narrow street. We went inside our hotel, thinking that was the end of it. But no. From the window of the breakfast room where we met up with the others, I could see the man lounging against the building across the street, smoking a cigarette, waiting. And waiting. And, cigarette tip now glowing in the dusk, still waiting.

My grandmother and I couldn't go to our room, because I didn't want him to see us crossing the hall through the glass hotel entrance and then see our room light up right at the front of the hotel. It was no doubt paranoid of me, but I didn't want him to know we were right there in that street-level room, the one with all the windows across the front of the building.

My brother-in-law, a take-charge and protective attorney, wanted to go out and send him on his way, but I asked him not to, because I was sure the man would leave. Eventually, he did, but only after he had waited almost an hour, time we had filled with talking, writing postcards, and calling home on the only phone we could use in the building. That was a lot of cigarettes for him, and a lot of false hope.

By American rules, his pursuit was ridiculous. I'd done nothing to encourage him. I was even out with my grandmother, for Pete's sake! But by French rules? Maybe things weren't so clear-cut. I had returned his look, however briefly, probably smiling a bit with discomfort and embarrassment. I was obviously very aware of him, snatching occasional peeks. I had even followed him into his checkout line, virtually shouting my interest. (At least, this is how I've tried to piece it together from his perspective.) So he followed me home and waited for me to join him. He was no doubt perplexed why I never did.

Social rules are, indeed, different in France, and I now believed what I had read: eye contact is powerful and can even be the first step to an affair. Maybe I'm flattering myself, but I'm quite sure that, had I wanted a quick affair with a lean brown-eyed Frenchman who chain smoked cigarettes and wore a leather sports-team jacket, I could have had one.

We made it through the rest of our stay without any more noticeable Looks, which I might be offended about if I were vainer. As it was, I was relieved not to have those smoldering stares directed at me. My staid Midwestern frumpiness could not handle the heat. Instead, my grandmother and I simply enjoyed our visit and, after a week, headed back to real life, where the social rules made sense, where we could smile at people, say hello to strangers, chat to locals as we shopped, and no one locked eyes with the burning strength of a laser.

I must admit, however, that the whole time we were in Paris, I did not see women with gray hair, so maybe my sister was on to something. There were lots of unlikely apricot and auburn tints, but no gray, except on the oldest women and a number of men. I also saw only one other French twist while we were in Paris. It was at the airport and was on an American tourist.

8
Genital Shock

"The French"—that monolithic body representing the nation as a whole, so often discussed in culture books—love the unusual, the unexpected, the cutting-edge, according to what I'd read. It's important to catch people's interest, surprise them, to challenge them intellectually. Just about the worst thing you can do to others, my research indicated, is to bore them. This love of pushing the envelope leads to some jarring juxtapositions, and they're intentional. A giant vulva sculpture in Rodin's lovely old mansion. The modern glass pyramid jutting up in the center of the sedately historic Louvre complex. Or the entire Pompidou Center, an inside-out, hulking industrial box that looms over venerable old structures such as the Gothic Saint-Merri Church.

I never went to the Pompidou Center with my grandmother, and Emily and I only made it as far as the fantastic fountain outside the building. My sister and her family had talked about how gloriously weird the modern art museum was, though, so Micki and I visited, to round out the art museum troika after our visits to the Louvre and the Musée d'Orsay.

The métro delivered us quite close to the Pompidou building, and as we neared, we saw bright ventilation pipes, heating pipes, water pipes, everything attached to the outside of the building, and each kind painted in a vivid color—red, green, blue, white—to draw attention to them. The bizarre, cartoon-like sculptures in the Picasso Fountain next to the building were also in crayon-bright primary colors, grotesquely warped and exaggerated figures that looked like Picasso's work in 3D.

Now, I can appreciate the absurd when it happens naturally in life and it amuses, but I don't like having it forced on me. I couldn't help staring at the enormous red lips that squirted water, at the multi-colored reclining mermaid with her bulbous thrusting breasts (that also squirted water, naturally) and thinking the fountain was garish, ridiculous, and unappealing. I suppose it's all supposed to be very playful and shake up fuddy-duddy expectations of art (and it's not far from the Picasso Museum, so it is a conscious play on his work), but I *am* an artistic fuddy-duddy, hopelessly traditional, and I found much of it to be simply grotesque and, well, childish. The smiling white skull did nothing for me. Only the elephant's head with its blue and white stripes and other bright colors, with its squirting trunk, well, that was rather cute, but probably because I have a soft spot for elephants. And even it, like everything else, was crude and rough looking. The display in the fountain, at any rate, was a good preview of what we would find inside the museum, so I suppose it succeeded in that sense.

Micki and I, having circled half the huge building already, continued our trek and ended up in a giant rectangular plaza that sloped down toward the building, like a shallow amphitheater. A number of people had gathered to watch an entertainer at the bottom of the incline, but we weren't interested in the show. We were on a mission to get to the museum, curious to

*Mermaid figure in the Picasso Fountain next to the Pompidou Center.
The shooting water was turned off for the moment.*

see what was inside. We found the entrance to the building and entered a cavernous hall at ground level. It looked like a convention center, not an art museum.

Wandering a bit, we saw no signs indicating where we should go, so we followed some other people up the escalator to the next level (which overlooked the first), but still couldn't figure out where to go. (Such whimsy! Such playfulness! Hiding the entrance to the museum and not marking it!) Eventually, we found our way to some escalators on the *outside* of the building and rode those up to the fourth floor. We cautiously entered the building again, but all we saw were stark white walls and no sign of a typical museum. There were two large, strange, witchlike hodge-podge sculptures (made of bits of rubbish) hanging on the wall, but unlike the Halloween witches we were familiar with, these emphasized the crotchal regions. Considering this welcome, I can't say we weren't warned about what was to come.

We wandered farther down the white halls and eventually found an opening into a room. Posted at the opening was a warning that the contents of the room might not be suitable for children, which we should have recognized as a sign that it probably wouldn't be suitable for us, either. The first thing we saw in the room was a line of photographs of a woman in various poses, emphasizing, as I recall, her nipples. They were all black-and-white photos, and all of this nude woman. Then there was a huge, wiry-dark-hair-like basket hanging from the ceiling. Supposedly, the artist hadn't known what he was going to make when he started—supposedly he didn't even know the weaving technique and learned it as he went along—but he ended up with a very sexual, womb-like structure that was also very weird.

I know there were other exhibits in the room that were equally shocking and disturbing, but the only other thing I remember well is a film projected against the wall we had entered through, which showed an act of sexual intercourse up close and enlarged. I have no idea how they placed the camera where they must have between the bodies, but it was virtually at the point of contact, so the film was just a close-up of the, um, interacting genitalia.

"This is pornography!" Micki hissed in shock, and we left the room not the least bit convinced that we had just witnessed "art." I looked later on a museum map and saw that the name of this first room was "Genital Shock."

The next room we entered had ghoulish dark stick-like figures in straight-backed chairs staring at a film projected on the wall. The film showed a naked woman hula hooping a ring of barbed wire, and as it circled her body, it pierced and ripped her skin so she became ever more wounded and bloody. The room was supposed to be a reminder of the Holocaust, if I remember correctly. We weren't moved by this display, either.

The next room we entered was quite dark and showed four films simultaneously. Three of the films were performance art. Starting from the left (where we entered) was an apple-shaped obese woman happily spinning around, dancing, jumping on and off a bench. (My memory is dim, but she must have been nude—all the other women were.) The next film showed a naked woman taking a live chicken, chopping its head off, and then holding the twitching bird by its legs in front of her body so the blood ran out and pooled between her legs.

The third film was another naked woman who papier-mâchéed herself bit by bit before the camera, applying some paper with her hands and rolling around in it at other times. The fourth film was just performance footage of Elvis. I think he might have been singing "Love Me Tender," but my brain had gone into a sort of shock, so I'm not sure about that now. All the films were black-and-white. They stunned us at the time, and I've been struggling ever since trying to determine whether they were supposed to be some group commentary, interacting somehow, or whether they were just placed together as weird pieces of performance art. The "odd man out," though, that Elvis film, makes me think that somehow they were supposed to work together and provide some great insight. That insight, I'm afraid, eluded Micki and me, and we were not able to see the display's artistic value (although we did eventually get the giggles). Hopelessly old-fashioned, hopelessly straightlaced Lutherans, that's what we were.

We breezed through the rest of that floor, not seeing anything remotely appealing, then decided we should go up a level to see the big-name artists, such as Picasso. We walked through it all quickly, and—although it will brand me as an artistic ignoramus—I can say that I did not see a single thing in that museum that I would like to have in my own house. I'd happily relocate most of the contents of the Musée d'Orsay or the Orangerie to my walls (all those lovely Impressionist works), but the modern art collection is safe from me.

After escaping from the Pompidou (getting out of the building was just about as baffling as getting into it had been), we zigged and zagged our way to the Place des Vosges. We were walking through the Marais district, and I had hoped that we would see lots of Orthodox Jews, clad in black with the skull caps and prayer fringes and locks, as Emily and I had seen three years earlier. But, no, we trudged all the way to the Place des Vosges and did not see a single Orthodox Jew, that we were aware of, at least. Coming as we did from a rural, white-bread part of the United States, the sight of devoted Jewish scholars would have been intriguing and exotic for us. We had to content ourselves with the knowledge that we were in the Jewish quarter, with Jewish stores and restaurants, even if we didn't see evidence of the faithful, themselves.

And then, the Place des Vosges itself was a bit of a letdown. It's supposed to be so beautiful, uniform and harmonious, a highlight of Parisian architecture, but it was kind of boring. I suppose it didn't help that there was some sort of construction in the middle blocking our view of the whole, but, frankly, I didn't think it was worth the effort to get to it. By that time, it was late enough that Victor Hugo's museum house was closed, and we didn't even bother going to the far end of the square to check that out. Of course, we were dog-tired by that point, so we weren't looking for any extra steps. Instead, we left the square and went around the corner to the Bastille site in search of the métro. The line we wanted was closed, but it was no problem to find an alternate route home.

It was funny, though, walking underground to get to our train, because in the crowd coming toward us was a tall, thin man with his head jutting forward, who looked and walked like the food critic Anton Ego from *Ratatouille*, that charming, animated tale of a rat that wants to be a chef. A person could do much worse than to base their introduction to Paris on that film, I mused. It showed the architecture, the obsession with food, the rigid social stratification, the style of dress, some of the major landmarks. Yes, it could serve as an introduction to the city, especially for those not old enough or modern enough for the *Amélie* version, which faithfully reveals the day-to-day life of a whimsical waitress and the people she works with, but also displays a lot of skin and activity that earns its R-rating. *Amélie* is also a delightful film, but it would be at least as enjoyable without all the sex images. Just a very few adjustments would make it a much more comfortable fit for us old-fashioned types. But those same adjustments, glossing over the sex acts and the sex drives and the sexual loneliness, would make it a whole lot less French, too.

At least with *Amélie*, I could see the attraction of the film and of the gamin-charming lead actress, Audrey Tautou, as well. The ongoing national enthusiasm for Jerry Lewis, however, completely eludes me. I'm truly baffled how the buffoon-ish Lewis convinces so many French people that his films are deep and that he is funny. I admit, I'm no Jerry Lewis scholar, but I did see some of his films on Saturday afternoons at the local theater when I was growing up, and what I remember from them is overdone slapstick, overacted idiocy, and lots of stupid faces. About all I can say about Jerry Lewis films (or my memory of them) is that at least we were spared seeing him in sex scenes. No close-ups of genitals or intercourse. No naked women dancing in circles or killing chickens or rolling around in what looked like toilet paper.

When it's all said and done, though, I'm sure I'd rather watch an old Elvis film.

9
Losing Their Heads

A spirit of revolution, of rebellion, threads through French history like the veins on the sides of my knees. While I know only the barest outlines of major historical events (I have a terrible memory for names and dates, which rather limits what bits of history I retain), even I am familiar with the main points of the French Revolution—widespread hunger, overspent treasury, growing discontent with the monarchy, popular uprising, "Let them eat cake," royal imprisonment, beheadings galore—and Paris was the epicenter of those events.

Many Americans are also familiar with a different Paris rebellion, usually mistaking it as part of the French Revolution, but it was a separate, later example of revolutionary fervor that most of us wouldn't even know about if it weren't for musical theater. The later, smaller event was the Paris Uprising of 1832 (also called the June Rebellion), as portrayed in Victor Hugo's *Les Misérables*, which I've never read, so I'm really referring to the Cameron Mackintosh musical version.

This uprising was an anti-monarchist insurrection that aimed to overthrow the recently established constitutional monarchy and reestablish a republic. (So much for all the bloodshed of the French Revolution in the 1790s. Here they were, back with a monarchy.) Unlike the French Revolution, this rebellion failed to gain wide public support, and this round of monarchy would survive for sixteen more years until the rise of the Second Republic. Back to *Les Mis*, though, as all viewers of the musical know (along with several readers who actually finished the book), many of the insurgents faced bloody battles with troops at street barricades on the night of June 5 to 6, 1832.

My personal experience with this event involves the story after the battle and is doubtless informed more by *Les Mis* than by textbook history, especially as I've never studied it. Not to compare my bravery with that of the insurgents, but I *have* taken a peek at (and a sniff of) the Paris sewers, specifically, that section of the huge under-street drainage system that is open as a museum. My little Emily, a doll-toting, pink-and-purple-dressed girl, was not interested in seeing the city sewer system, but I was, and—much like the French monarchs—I had the deciding vote over everything we did.

As many people know because of the phenomenal success of *Les Mis*, Victor Hugo was friends with a Paris sewer inspector and used that friend's intimate knowledge of the underground labyrinth as part of his novel. In the story, the aging hero, Jean Valjean, rescues the young rebel Marius after he has been shot at the barricades and, sloshing through the dark tunnel system, carries him to safety. I realize that the actual insurrection does not loom large historically, but I knew that Emily would someday see *Les Mis* and thought that a reference point for that heroic undertaking through the sewers might deepen her understanding and appreciation of the story, of the bravery, unselfishness, and love demonstrated by Jean Valjean.

She was not enthusiastic when I shared my plans.

"We're going to *what?*" She wrinkled her nose. "I don't want to go through the sewers."

I played my monarch's trump card. "Too bad. We're going."

She sighed. "Will it stink?"

I thought of the guidebook descriptions advising readers that they might want to change their clothes after the tour.

"No, not much at all. The system is for all the wastewater, showers and washing machines and stuff."

In stark contrast to most sights in Paris, there was no line to buy tickets at *Les Égoûts*, as the sewer museum is called, but we were not the only tourists there on that overcast March morning. We descended the steps near the Pont de l'Alma along the Seine near the Eiffel Tower and plunged into the dank underworld of Paris, where the streets above have corresponding wastewater tunnels below, and the subterranean passages are even named for the streets, creating a shadow city that mirrors the City of Light.

The whole tunnel system is extensive—over 1,300 miles in all—but just a short portion is open to form the museum. The tour section is well-lit and dry, with rooms showcasing displays that range from mannequins dressed as sewer workers to the history of *Les Misérables*, including maps that depict the accuracy of Victor Hugo's account of the tunnel system.

A walled-in river of brown waste and runoff water ran below our elevated walkways. Emily and I visited Paris too late—years late—for the old-version sewer tours, where rowboats floated visitors through the very muck. As it was, we were comfortably removed from anything strongly unpleasant. Perhaps we were there on a good day, but the smell was not even bad. We've walked along city streets that had far stronger sewer odors.

The visit to the Paris sewers was hardly a highlight of the trip, but it was an interesting side note for me, filling out the

Paris sewer tunnel

picture of what happens to the early morning gutter-flushing bursts of water I had seen above. (Small hydrants are built into many curbsides to provide the cleaning water.) The sewer visit was a brief encounter with history and literature through civil engineering.

I did not take Micki to the sewer museum, even though it was close to our hotel. We had far too many other things to see and do during our brief stay in Paris, such as visit landmarks that brought to life the French Revolution and the irresistible story of Marie Antoinette.

I suppose the figure of Marie Antoinette appealed to me in part because she was a Habsburg, one of that long and powerful line of Austrian rulers, and I was familiar with them from my college German studies and then, later, from when I lived in Austria. The Habsburgs ruled for some six hundred years, not just over present-day Austria, but much of central Europe and, through the Spanish line of the family, over lands spanning the globe. Probably the best known ruler of the Austrian Habsburgs was Empress Maria Theresa, who reigned for forty years and produced sixteen children, including number fifteen, little Maria Antonia, who would later be known as Marie Antoinette.

Born an archduchess, Marie Antoinette was overlooked as a political pawn until several of her older sisters died of smallpox. At that point, she was the only girl in the family left to marry off. Forget love matches and romantic happily-ever-afters—Marie's mother, the empress, believed in cementing political alliances through marriage, and when the time came, Marie Antoinette was promised in marriage to the future King Louis XVI of France. They would have rocky going, even before the revolution and their violent deaths.

The young couple married by proxy in Vienna in 1770, with one of Marie's brothers standing in for young Louis. Marie was fourteen; her distant bridegroom was fifteen. A couple of weeks later, an Austrian delegation transported her toward France, and they handed her over to a French delegation on an island in the Rhine River. The next week, she met her young husband, and they were soon joined in a ceremonial wedding at the Palace of Versailles.

That night they were led to their "ritual bedding," but— almost complete strangers to each other—they failed to, shall we say, unite their dynasties as expected. For whatever reason (possibly a mutual cluelessness about the process), they apparently did not consummate the marriage until seven years later, after Marie Antoinette's empress mother sent Marie's brother the Holy Roman Emperor to investigate why there had been no heir yet.

I could not help wondering, first, how people knew that the "ritual bedding" had been a complete flop, and second, how incredibly embarrassing it would be to have your mom send your big brother to grill you about your sex life. I know that I am projecting modern sensibilities onto this situation, but doesn't that seem a bit much? I suppose that after sixteen children of her own, Maria Theresa was not shy about bedroom matters. And, given the earthiness of the time, possibly no one else was sensitive about them either, but the thought of such an interrogation makes me cringe.

Throughout our visit in France, Micki and I periodically walked the path of Marie Antoinette's tragic life, but in largely reverse order. We had started at the Conciergerie a couple of days before, the hulking gray stone structure, a former palace and current judicial building that was used as a prison in Marie's day. After her arrest, she was held in captivity about fourteen months (the last two in the Conciergerie), which was considerably longer than her husband the king, who lasted only five months before losing his head.

Marie Antoinette had never been very popular at the French court (there was just too much suspicion of her as an Austrian), but it was only later, when the costs of several wars strained state finances, and the poor became even poorer, that the people of France turned violently against their monarchy. While she probably didn't understand the full extent of the people's suffering, it is well documented that Marie Antoinette never uttered what is possibly the most misattributed line of history: Let them eat cake.

Nonetheless, it's indisputable that the people were still without bread, and on Aug. 13, 1792, the entire royal family was imprisoned. The king was beheaded Jan. 21, 1793. On Oct. 16 of that same year, after a trial of largely trumped-up, often lurid charges (including false accusations of incest with her son), Marie Antoinette was loaded onto a crude two-wheeled open cart and trundled over the bumpy cobblestone streets along the Seine to her death.

Micki and I followed the same route and may have trod on the very stones Marie rode over. She would have been wheeled past the Louvre (also a former palace) to the Place de la Revolution, the huge public space that is now called the much more peaceful Place de la Concorde, or "Harmony Square." The square is enormous, ringed by busy streets and luxury hotels, and it's hard to imagine it packed with a blood-thirsty mob, baying for her death. But so it must have been. Accounts of the time report that Marie Antoinette maintained her dignity despite the lack of a royal gown and the loss of her hair (cut short to better aim the blade at the back of her neck). Wearing a plain white dress, she ascended a wooden platform—possibly, I continue to hope, where the towering Egyptian obelisk now stands—apologized to the executioner for accidentally stepping on his foot, and knelt to her death. Her body was dumped into an unmarked grave. Before the so-called Reign of Terror ended the next year, some 40,000 "enemies of the revolution" had been killed.

Only later in the week, our last day in Paris, did Micki and I venture to the palace at Versailles, where Marie had come as a fourteen-year-old girl to wed her practically unknown prince. We were up at seven (an early morning for us, given the late hours we had been keeping) to catch the train to Versailles. After the ride, we took a short walk from the station to the palace. We didn't need a map, but just followed the hordes of tourists streaming that way. We arrived at the château at nine and were able to walk in after a very short wait. Our self-guided tour of the palace went smoothly, once we barged past the various tour groups clogging the route.

Those tour groups were like dumb herds of cattle, shuf-fling from one room to the next, blocking any normal traffic flow as they stood in clumps trying to hear their braying guides in the din. We pushed through clusters of all nation-alities, it seemed—Spanish, Japanese, Italian, French—and finally, because of our early arrival, we were able to burst through to freedom on the front side of the tour bus crowds.

We really picked up steam, then, to avoid being surrounded by the masses again.

Despite our hurry, a couple parts of the palace really stand out in my memory. One is the Hall of Mirrors, not just because the Treaty of Versailles was signed there, ending World War I, but because of something I'd read in Neal Stephenson's novel *The Confusion*, set when the fabled Sun King, Louis XIV, held court there. In the story, winter was so cold at Versailles that the inhabitants half froze, and toilet facilities were so limited that people used the halls to relieve themselves. The book's main character, Eliza, walked down palace corridors littered with steaming piles of feces, a vision that rather robs both the place and the period of their romance and elegance.

While the substitute latrine corridors certainly did not include the exalted Hall of Mirrors, I couldn't help picturing the hall that way—just briefly—when I viewed it. Frankly, that fleeting image humanized the formal hall and made it not just beautiful and impressive but interesting, a reminder that people had actually lived in the palace and it hadn't always been a museum. In our clean and pampered lives, it's so easy to overlook how crude and dirty things were not that long ago, even at the center of the civilized world.

The other part of the palace I remember fairly well is the sleeping section, with separate bedchambers for the king and queen, but with an adjoining door between them. The queen's room was feminine—light and floral—and the king's was bold red and gold. Again the questions flitted through my head. How often did the king use his private passage to visit the queen? Did she have any say in the matter? Did she ever go visit him? Did they ever encounter any surprises when opening the doors that connected their rooms? And I wanted to know whether the royal couple ever had any real privacy.

Their bedrooms, after all, had been designed largely as public rooms, as well as places to sleep and cavort. The king

Hall of Mirrors at the Palace of Versailles

The king's ceremonial bedchamber at Versailles

held small audiences as he dressed, as did the queen, and even worse, the queen had to give birth in public there. Surely, by comparison, even the paparazzi-plagued royalty of today have considerable privacy. I doubt anyone attended the birth of Britain's little Prince George who wasn't related to Will or Kate or who didn't have to be there for medical reasons. Modern monarchy may still be confined to a fish bowl, but at least it offers the possibility of privacy, a few places to hide from the viewers. And I'm quite certain that the situation has improved greatly on the bathroom front.

After our flying early morning visit through the main palace, Micki and I walked through the vast gardens toward the Grand Trianon, a slightly less formal palace, smaller than the main one, that the king and his favorites could retreat to. It was a novel experience to wander through the gardens on foot. When I had been there with my grandmother, we had ridden one of the motorized wagons (a so-called "garden train") to see the main sights of the estate, and when I was there with Emily, it was cold and she wasn't remotely interested in shrubbery, so I don't think we even saw the gardens, other than maybe a quick overview from the terrace behind the palace.

But Micki and I trod the gravel paths bordered by shrubs to get to the other main buildings of the estate. I would dearly love to see the palace and the garden as they were in their heyday, peopled by the French court in all its finery, courtiers meeting for their intrigues and rendezvous. The setting is there; it's just my imagination that's deficient. I'm sure, though, that if I could have my wish and temporarily travel back through time, Micki and I would be identified immediately as peasants and probably thrown into prison. I don't know why we would be jailed. I suspect that being non-aristocratic, non-fashionable, and non-subservient would have been reason enough. Maybe Micki's bling would win her a reprieve, but I would be doomed. I'm a peasant through and through. As baffling as French protocol can be today, it must have been infinitely worse at the height of the French court, and Micki and I would do everything wrong.

We made it down a fairly straight shot to the Grand Trianon, but our efficiency bit us—the building didn't open until noon. So, we walked onward to the smaller-yet palace, the Petit Trianon, which was Marie Antoinette's retreat from the pressures of court life at the big palace. It, too, was closed until noon. On we walked, then, to a part of the estate I had never visited before (not even on a garden train), to the hamlet. It was, of course, closed until noon.

We were the only ones at this remote edge of the park at this time, so we sat on a wooden barricade for half an hour eating apples until the hamlet opened. But what a treat it turned out to be. This was Marie's retreat from her retreat, the private little farm where she could play at being a peasant, a farm girl, a milk maid. Dotted with half-timbered buildings and artistic ponds, connected by winding paths, it was a refuge of peace, beauty, and tranquility. We *loved* it. We loved the geese, the pig pen, the cottages, the mill, every part of it. Marie had had the mini-village built as a reconstruction of a true country hamlet, and it may well have seemed as artificial at the time as Disneyland's Main Street does to us, but it utterly charmed and delighted Micki and me. Other than the lack of peasants running around (besides us)—and, of course, a lack of foul smells, which I'm sure abounded back in the day—it seemed authentic to us.

After wandering around the entire hamlet, we returned to the other two palaces, the Petit and then the Grand Trianon, both very grand and gorgeous, but which couldn't help but disappoint after the attractions of the hamlet. It was a stunning contrast of the simple and picturesque against the gilded and impressive, and—small-town girl and country girl that

The mill in Marie Antoinette's faux hamlet at Versailles

we were—we preferred the simple version. The palaces at Versailles were designed to intimidate, and that they did in spades, but for actually living, the fake hamlet was far more appealing.

We hiked back through the gardens and saw the endlessly long, intersecting waterways of the Grand Canal, which, I'm afraid, also failed to fire our enthusiasm. Yes, life was different back before television and the Internet, before easy communication and transportation, but floating around in a rowboat on a couple of elongated ditches frankly doesn't sound that exciting. Perhaps we were just tired and failed to appreciate the diversion that the Grand Canal offered.

We eventually rounded the main palace, still trudging across expanses of gravel. If all the graveled paths are period appropriate, how did their old-time shoes weather the beating? Did the delicate slippers constantly rip? Were people stopping every six yards to fish stones out of their footwear, as Micki and I were? Somewhere on one of the paths, I had managed to stumble a bit, nothing serious, but it would cause some problems for me later. I was wearing sturdy hiking sandals. How could ladies even stroll wearing dainty heeled shoes? Maybe they were hauled everywhere on litters.

We reached the train station by two and were back at the hotel by three, after walking almost constantly the five hours we had been in Versailles. It was a relief to be back in our room so early in the day, where we could rest a bit and plan while it was still afternoon, instead of late at night, as was the usual case. We had visited everything on our "must see" list for Paris, and after five exhausting days, the many items on the "would be nice" list were a lot less enticing than they had seemed at the start of the trip. The visit to the department store, the fashion show, the flea market, the cooking class—they could wait for another trip. After all, as Sabrina says in the movie of that same name, "Paris is always a good idea." We just need to get the timing right.

With a chance to catch up on housekeeping details, we lined up our shuttle ride to the airport for the next morning and quickly caught up on email and Facebook. We were back in our domain, with the peasants, with our modern conveniences and comforts, and we were happy to be there.

10
Cheesed Off

It took a while before I mustered the courage to enter a restaurant in Paris. I was cowed by the French reputation for food persnicketiness, by their legendarily intimidating waiters, and by their foreign dining customs. My travel companions and I have always been happy with simple food, with fruit and cheese, bread and pastries—street food that we find tasty, filling, quick, and economical. Who wants to take the time, the money, and the ego hit that come with a visit to a traditional restaurant?

I admit, some aspects of the food-centered culture in France are a pleasure, even for us less sophisticated types. My grandmother and I loved visiting the local street market, with its rows of neatly organized displays. Such variety! Such specialization! A single vendor there had at least twenty-one different tubs of gleaming olives, each of a different kind. And the cheese displays! They were works of art, featuring an assortment of dozens of dairy options, from the ripe and runny to firm and fruity.

Of course, it's not possible to discuss French cheese

without referring to the famous quote from former French president Charles de Gaulle: "How can anyone govern a nation that has two hundred and forty-six different kinds of cheese?" From the information I've run across, the actual number these days is somewhere between 300 and 400. That's a lot of cheese.

Given the "local food" ethos of France, I was surprised to see so many junk food joints there—that didn't fit with their image at all. There is no shortage of McDonald's restaurants (McDo), KFC restaurants, and Burger Kings—even candy bar vending machines. But that's not the national standard, of course.

The national ideal epitomizes the slow food movement: cooks should carefully choose the freshest ingredients, carefully prepare them in the most flavorful way, carefully display the food on the plate—or plates, since we're probably talking about multiple courses. Pair the foods with the most appropriate wines. Eat the food in the most discriminating way—reverentially, if it's good. Discuss everything about the food, from the selection at the market, if cooking it oneself, to a prolonged discussion of the offerings with a waiter in a restaurant. Don't rush the experience, but linger over it.

It all seems rather time-consuming for my tight tourist schedule, and, not really speaking French, I find the prospect of a detailed discussion terrifying. Better to stick with bread, fruit, and cheese in the room.

The first meal I had in any place truly French was with my grandmother in Paris. Our whole family group decided to go out together to a neighborhood *brasserie*, which looks an awful lot like *brassiere* but is a type of "relaxed" French restaurant (if there is such a thing) that is still traditional enough that it has white linens. Honestly, we didn't have the nerve to tackle a true French restaurant, one with the word "restaurant" in its name. The intimidation factor would be off the meter at one of those, and so would the prices. Certainly beyond my budget, anyway. The term *brasserie*, though, comes from the old French word for "brewery," which sounds a lot more comfortable and affordable than a restaurant, but it was still a long way from a beer garden.

We had walked by this neighborhood *brasserie* many times on our way to and from our hotel, so it was the obvious choice when we ventured out for our white-table-cloth dining experience. Although there no longer appeared to be any brewery associated with this place, *brasseries* typically include a nice selection of beers on tap. Not that we planned to drink beer. We weren't in Germany. We would do the French thing and drink wine with our dinner. That much we knew. We just weren't sure how to handle the rest of dinner the French way. Fortunately, we ate at a rural American suppertime (around 6 p.m.), so we ran very little chance of having a crowded roomful of locals to witness our attempts.

We gathered in the breakfast room of our hotel and strolled in the gloomy early March dusk to the *brasserie*. The waiter greeted us stiffly at the door and then moved an already-settled man from his table at the window so that we could have his spot. We, of course, did not want to displace the poor man, but we had previously seen in our own little breakfast room that even the mild-mannered waitress there did not hesitate to move people from tables she did not deem suitable for them. In the breakfast room case, two men had taken a table that seated four. Scolding, the waitress descended on them and moved them to a table for two, so they could be properly cramped, as the rest of us were.

I actually have a good bit of sympathy with this efficient use of limited table and seating space. Long after the breakfast rearrangement in France, I was in a Culver's restaurant in Iowa (a fast-food hamburger chain where customers seat themselves) and noticed that among my fellow patrons, a single person had taken a booth for four, there were just two people in a booth for five, and a group of three people had taken one of the corner booths that easily seat six to eight customers. That type of heedless space hoggery takes place all the time in America, even when the restaurant is crowded and customers are looking for someplace to sit. We believe that physical space, like every other resource, is our birthright to take as much of as we please. I would very much have liked to have had a French waiter or waitress there officiously scolding the blatant space hogs and removing them to appropriately sized tables. Maybe Culver's and other self-seating eating establishments should consider that. (I was by myself, I'll note, in a booth for two, the smallest kind available.)

But, back in Paris, the customer in the *brasserie* was at a tiny table for two, not out of line at all, reading and smoking and minding his own business. Still, he got booted to the corner of the room so the waiter could shove several of the tiny tables together to accommodate our party and display us in the window by the street. I think we became a kind of advertising. *See, all you passersby? This is where you want to eat in Paris! These are Americans here in the window having a good time!* I'm not sure we would have attracted any diners beyond other Americans, but maybe that's all they were hoping for from us.

We received a menu labeled "American" for language, and from the limited offerings, most of us selected either the beef tips or the chicken, with my teenaged niece and nephew going rogue and choosing the hamburger and the duck. We had to order drinks, as well, of course, and I knew enough from my research that I was afraid to choose the wrong thing (a Coke, for example) and anxious to make a good impression on my waiter. (Yes, in France, you are advised to establish a good relationship with your waiter—the onus is on *you* to make nice to *him*—and get him on your side.) Here are my own words of advice, based on considerable reading, which

I eventually cut from the book I was working on because of space limitations:

To really fit in and please your server, ask about the various dishes and discuss their merits. (Do it as if you are asking for a favor, excusing yourself first, to really make a good impression.) This shows that you appreciate the seriousness of the decision and your waiter's knowledge of the subject. Well, that's what the French do, anyway. We visitors with limited language skills are perhaps better off throwing ourselves at the mercy of our waiter and not attempting a full discussion.

It sounds ridiculous, turned about and servile in the United States, but we were in Paris, and that's what I did. I asked the frosty waiter in my careful French, *"Pouvez-vous recommander un vin rouge?,"* and he suggested a glass of red that was just fine. (I'm no more a wine snob than a food snob. Any old plonk is just fine by me.) My grandmother and my nephew decided to split an order of *escargots*, which the rest of us were happy to pass on. They were not put off at all by the snails swimming in garlic butter, but the special fork and shell tongs that came with them required some experimentation. Try as they might, they just couldn't get a good grip on those slippery round shells, which meant they weren't able to dig the snail meat out with the little fork. Eventually, the waiter came over and demonstrated that they had been trying to clamp the shells backwards and needed to flip the apparatus around. What can we say? Somehow, we'd never run across snail tongs in Iowa.

Soon after we'd ordered, we looked at a French version of the menu, picked up from a nearby table, just out of curiosity. My sister, who had studied a bit of French in high school, glanced through the French-language listings and, with a gasp and a start, found the hamburger her daughter had ordered. She looked at me in horror.

"Doesn't *cheval* mean horse?"

"I think so. Let me look it up." I pulled out my phrasebook and thumbed through the small dictionary in the back. Yep, horse.

"The hamburgers are made with horse meat," she said, looking slightly sick. My niece declared that she did not want the horse hamburger, so when the waiter brought us our drinks, my sister informed him that the hamburger order needed to be changed to chicken. He seemed to understand, but his English wasn't any firmer than our French, so we weren't sure.

A short bit later we wanted to double check, so we approached the waiter, who was standing back by the bar, and told him in clear pidgin English that we did not want *cheval* hamburger; we wanted another chicken: *trois poulet* (holding up three fingers). The waiter appeared to be telling my sister that there was no *cheval* in the hamburger, but we had seen it on the menu. *No hamburger. Chicken*, we repeated.

When our food arrived, we all welcomed our plates except my niece, because the waiter delivered not one but *two* plates with hamburgers on them. We now had seven dinners for six diners, and two of them were hamburgers with a semi-cooked egg on top, *not* the chicken we had changed the order to. (Where the second horse hamburger entered the picture, I have no idea.) I don't remember exactly what happened next—I know we sent the two hamburgers back, the waiter probably told us it was not horse (*pas cheval!*), and my niece got by with bits of other people's dinners.

We were convinced that the "American" version of the menu just hid the origin of the meat from us because the French owners knew that hamburger-loving Americans wouldn't order the dish, if we knew it came from a horse. We thought that the waiter didn't change the order perhaps because it would do the Americans good to try horse hamburger. Or maybe it was just a bad restaurant. My nephew, who had ordered duck, received a plate of salmon. When we got back to our hotel, we discovered we had been overcharged, too, but in the confusion of paying a combined bill, we had missed that.

Years later, when my glacial progress on the French-for-tourists book I was writing finally got me to investigate food terminology, I discovered that the French cooking term *à cheval* means something along the lines of "on horseback" and refers to a dish with an egg "riding" on top. The semi-cooked eggs on the hamburgers, in our case. Sometimes a little knowledge really can be worse than none. No horse hamburger. The waiter was right, and our great story went out the window. We were just another bunch of clueless Americans.

The day after our horse hamburger experience, we tried eating out again. My grandmother and I were in Versailles. After touring the grounds in the little garden train, we stopped at a crêperie in the village for lunch. We ended up ordering the same combination for our meal: a salad crêpe, a ham, egg, and cheese crêpe, and a dessert crêpe to round things off. The salad crêpe was salad greens, walnuts, and a vinaigrette dressing in a savory crêpe, unusual but very tasty, and good for tiding us over until our main course.

When the next plate arrived, my grandmother and I were both surprised because our ham-and-cheese filling was topped with an apricot half, which I did not remember from the item description in the menu, but there could be much that either did not get translated or that I had missed in my reading of French. Apricot and ham would go together just fine, though, so we shrugged and grabbed our silverware to dig in. What a surprise we had, then, when our apricots leaked deep orange liquid throughout our crêpes, and the first bite confirmed that the half-sphere of fruit was, in fact, a raw egg yolk.

We both paused and looked dubiously at our plates. They swam in orange yolk. Looking at each other, we decided to soldier on, although the cold egg was awful. But we neither wanted to offend the restaurateur nor throw out the main part of our meal. I probably ate around what I could of the yolk, but there was no denying that the dish was a great disappointment. Our second foray into a true French eatery was not a rousing success.

French restaurants: 2, American tourists: 0

My grandmother and I managed to avoid any type of French restaurant for the remainder of our stay, until we were stuck at an airport hotel with the rest of our flight because of a day-long delay in departure. The dreaded "mechanical problems," we were told.

I'm not sure when the "mechanical problems" actually arose. We showed up at least four hours early to check in, and our flight had already been cancelled—not because of mechanical problems, but because our plane was taken over by the *previous* day's flight, which had been bumped to *our* day. We know this from my sister, because her family had been scheduled to leave on *that* flight, had been bumped to *our* plane the next day, but they couldn't stay the extra day and had found an alternate way home. One wonders how many days this went on, and how it could possibly be profitable for the airline to keep delaying flights for a day and having to house and feed planeload after planeload of passengers.

While an extra day in Paris sounds fabulous, it really wasn't. It wasn't in Paris, for starters, but out in Roissy, the suburb of about 2,500 people next to Charles de Gaulle airport, and which has no direct connections to Paris. If we wanted to revisit the city, we would first need to take a bus to the airport and catch the métro there. It seemed like too much work (especially for my frail grandmother), when we'd already said our goodbyes to Paris and were mentally and emotionally ready to go home. Plus, we'd spent out our euros and didn't want to withdraw more. So our exciting-sounding "layover in Paris" was really a boring day hanging around an isolated hotel complex with no money to spend, even when we did eventually wander into the village, which was a good slow hike off into the distance. But we did get a couple of decent meals out of the deal.

After the flight cancellation, we were directed to a shuttle bus to take us to a hotel, along with everyone else on the same flight to the United States. Dinner was provided for us in the hotel restaurant that evening, a buffet of salads, appetizers, and desserts, and the waitstaff would bring us a plate of roasted chicken and rice. We were among the first in the extensive dining room, gladly served ourselves at the generous buffet, then waited patiently for our main course. The room filled up. Everyone around us received their chicken. We waited, looking for our waitress. People left other tables, new ones came in, and *they* received their main course. No sign of our waitress. Or our food.

After at least an hour of waiting for our main course, my well-mannered grandmother approached the man overseeing the buffet, showed him where we were sitting, and asked him, "Excuse me, but where is our entrée?"

"Why, it is over there, *Madame*," he said, pointing to the buffet.

"No, our *entrée*," she emphasized.

"The *entrées* are over there, at the *buffet*," the man repeated haughtily.

Exasperated (and hungry), my little grandmother finally exploded, "Where's our chicken?!"

Oh! The chicken! He thought she had meant the *entrée*! (In France, it's the appetizer, the *entry* to a meal.) Well, the man investigated, determined that our waitress had abandoned our table to work a special party in another room, and he quickly remedied the oversight. We soon received our chicken. We had simply been lost in the staffing shuffle.

There are at least two morals to this story. 1) Make sure to use the French terms in French ways when speaking with French people. And, 2) there is a limit to how much time you should give the waiter to deliver courses. Even the notoriously slow French service should have taken far less time than we endured. And to really top things off, the chicken was all pink near the bone, and we left half our meat, because we weren't sure it was safe to eat.

I don't think I went to a real French restaurant (of any variety) when I was there with young Emily. Our Paris stay was shortened because of that weather delay on the way over, so our already packed schedule was stuffed even fuller as we tried to see everything we wanted. Emily was so intoxicated by Paris, so excited about her first trip abroad that she was aware of (a trip to Germany as a two-year-old was long forgotten), that she couldn't slow down to eat. I was lucky to get an occasional crêpe into her.

Emily and I finished off our French trip with two days and nights at Disneyland Paris, staying at the Hotel Cheyenne on the Disney property. That was my first encounter with Disney, so I have no idea how the American parks are, but I expected better from the hotel we stayed at. Our room was worn, dark, and poorly supplied, without facial tissues or toiletries. Half the light bulbs were out and needed to be replaced.

As if the interior gloom weren't bad enough, it was raining buckets our first day there, which had the sole advantage of keeping the crowds down. After a turn through the Universal Studios park, and then a dozen times through the perky hell of "It's a Small World" (no waiting!), we made it back to our hotel, dripping and cold, and then went to the on-site Western-themed restaurant for our supper. Breakfast and evening meals, after all, were included in our Disney package.

I was appalled. The European (largely French) families we saw there were every bit as ill-behaved as a group of American families might have been under the same circumstances. They hogged tables, piled on food from the buffet that they didn't eat, were loud, pushy, and obnoxious. It was curiously gratifying. I can't believe that the French food patrol (if there were such a thing, rather like the French Academy that polices the language to make sure that it stays sufficiently French, but with food) would allow the bland and mediocre dishes that were served in the Disney hotel. Most of it was awful.

I could understand why the other families were leaving heaps of uneaten food on their plates. What I didn't understand was why they had taken so much to begin with. (It was a buffet! They could go back as many times as they wanted to!) What a disappointment the food was, like bad hospital fare. It didn't begin to compete with the street food we had been eating for convenience's sake. And as for the meals we had in the Magic Kingdom itself, well, those were American fast food experiences, nothing to write home about and ridiculously expensive, but at least edible. I didn't fault those meals for not being "French" when they came from that bastion of American capitalism, the Disney Corporation.

I didn't enter a real French restaurant again until I was with Micki, on our last night in Paris. We had spent the day logging miles to and from and around Versailles, and we rewarded ourselves by enjoying our last evening in the capital of culture. We decided we would visit a local bistro, but which one was a puzzle. After wandering around checking out the possibilities, we chose one at a busy intersection with outdoor seating, where we had ample people-watching opportunities. We ordered a *kir* cocktail each, feeling oh-so-sophisticated, and for perhaps the first time, really relaxed while trying to experience Paris.

We sat at the edge of the patio, near a newspaper kiosk with the métro entrance not far away. Our local supermarket was down the block, and we noticed many bags and baskets of food being bustled by before us. An old man in a brown suit kept guard over the star-patterned intersection, where three streets more or less crossed. He nabbed passersby at the elbows and gave them advice (generally unwelcome), which we could interpret from where we sat: Carry your bag across the body for safety! Follow this route to get where you're going! Our vantage point allowed us to view locals hurrying home after work, as well as tourists shuffling around, often bemused and confused.

We'd really only wanted a pre-dinner drink. After leisurely observing the local activity, we returned to our room as evening approached because it was getting chilly and we wanted our jackets. It was our last night in Paris, though, so we decided to go out for dinner after all, returning to the same bistro, to the same table, and selecting steak, fries, wine and then *crème brûlée*. The food was fantastic, the atmosphere was fantastic, and our young buck waiter was handsome, funny, and mildly flirtatious, a welcome contrast to the frosty waiter my group had encountered years before in the Latin Quarter. I don't know whether service norms had changed in that time or whether it was just that the young waiter was more playful (much!!) than the older one had been. Or maybe his informality was because it was the August holiday time.

Our simple dinner was wonderful. The price, not so much. With a small extra tip (the price included a service charge), the total came to 56 euros for the two of us, something around $37 each, which might be cheap for a restaurant meal in Paris, but for me, it was a splurge.

Of course, there are much more expensive splurges in Paris. Many of them. One of the priciest must be the Jules Verne restaurant about halfway up on the Eiffel Tower. I couldn't come close to affording an actual visit (although I know people who have been there on an expense account), but I saw online that the cheapest set meal there was 90 euros ($120),

Typical French hotel breakfast, complete with fruit cocktail.

and that jumped to 125 euros ($166) with wine. Wine cost 35 euros?? Clearly, they're not serving plonk, there. (The Jules Verne restaurant offerings and prices do change periodically, so I will just discuss what was current when I checked.)

The à la carte prices were even worse: the cheapest appetizer was 52 euros ($69) for snails, the lobster appetizer was 92 euros ($122), and the desserts were all 26 euros (a mere $35). Well, that made it easy. If I were eating à la carte, I would skip the appetizers and go straight to dessert.

I have to point out that those were all discount prices on lunch, for weekdays. On the weekend, the same set menu for lunch jumped from 90 to 175 euros ($233), and the dinner menus started at an eye-popping 210 euros ($280). Such wild extravagance was not just beyond my comfort zone, but almost beyond my comprehension. How rich would I have to be before I would enjoy a meal I had paid that much for? And what sort of dress code would be required for a $280 meal (over $400, if I threw in wine)? *Per person!*

For all its fancy-pants elegance—it's on the *Eiffel Tower!!*—I'm not sure I would actually want to eat there. The menu listed a lot of duck *fois gras* and shellfish and things like veal kidneys or sweetbreads or something, which are way off my radar as a culturally sheltered Midwesterner raised on plentiful tuna casserole and sweet corn. One who couldn't even use snail tongs. If I hadn't already known it, awareness of this fancy restaurant and others like it would have convinced me that I could never be a high flier. I'm much happier sticking to street food, grocery store picnics, and the occasional $37 dinner out. The people in that glorified realm may as well be living on a different planet. To be fair, I'm pretty sure that not all patrons of the Jules Verne restaurant are rich as sin. Many tourists do it for a splurge, a special experience, and if I found the menu more appealing, I might even consider that myself some day (if I didn't have to dress up too much). As it is, though, I'd be happy enough to be able to press my nose against the window and look in, which is not very likely, given its location.

Once Micki and I had experienced our own lowly version of the French restaurant, and it was pleasant and tasty and comfortable, with a friendly waiter, we were primed to brave more restaurants as we ventured away from Paris to rural areas of the country. And we needed to brave them, because after we left our cozy location on rue Cler, we lost our easy access to a supermarket. No longer surrounded by convenient street food and shopping, we almost *had* to try restaurants, if we wanted to eat. And we did, mostly with success. I may never fully embrace the traditional French dining experience, but at least I had reached an uneasy truce with it, and Micki and I would not starve in the countryside.

But before moving on, we needed to pack and actually get out of the city.

Part II: On the Road

11
The Heart of France

Micki and I were up at seven our last morning in Paris. We ate apples for breakfast while we packed up, then went outside to wait for the airport shuttle in front of the hotel. Being overly cautious, as usual, we were ready far too early and had plenty of time to fetch croissants from the local bakery before the *navette* was scheduled to arrive.

While we stood on the street and savored our croissants, three police officers pulled up and walked into the hotel. They spoke with a very stylish, very upset little old lady, who seemed to be indicating that she had had some things stolen. She was white-haired, very proper and tidy in her skirt, blouse and jacket, with a purse and umbrella hanging from her arm. The officers walked her down the street to the police car and helped her in. The neighborhood was so peaceful, the street and hotel so quiet, that it was hard to imagine that she had really been a victim of theft. The clerk at the front desk certainly didn't think so, shaking his head doubtfully when we looked curiously at him, but I suppose he would have downplayed any real crime when communicating with tourists who were staying at the hotel. Not good for business, after all.

For the last time, with bittersweet pleasure, we admired the quaint charm of our neighborhood. I had read somewhere that the beauty of Paris is all the more impressive because it is all manmade, and that was so here. The narrow cobblestone street, now mostly a pedestrian zone. The mellow stone buildings with their wrought-iron window grills and window boxes spilling over with red geraniums. The bustling specialty food shops—the fish store, the cheese store, the fruit and vegetable store. Everything was small scale and real, touchable, not encased in plastic. We would miss the rich livability, the everyday prettiness of the street when we returned to our land of big-box stores and sterile commercialism.

Soon the van pulled up to take us to the airport. Our foreign driver (Vietnamese, I would guess) knew little English and spoke non-native French. When he asked where we were going, he mistook "Giverny" as "Germany," and I really don't think my pronunciation was that bad.

"*Non Alemagne*," I said (wrongly), or something similar. OK, he got that. "*Normandie*," I said, which he then understood.

He charged us each an extra two euros to take us directly to the car rental place, Avis ("ah-vee"). That was enough of a shakedown. We shouldn't have tipped him on top of it, but we did, because we are wimps and didn't want to appear rude. Oh, well. That makes up for the mother/daughter team from Kansas, whom we picked up just off the Champs-Élysées before heading to the airport.

They looked more than ready to go home, levering up their huge, overloaded suitcases and shoving them into the back of the van with help from the driver. They had started their trip in Ireland (driving), visited friends in London, and then spent something like five days or a week in Paris. Their experience hadn't been nearly as pleasant as ours had. They had seen quite a bit of rudeness, they said. Of course, they were staying in the really ritzy district, so maybe people *were* rude there. Or maybe the Kansas duo went into situations with the wrong attitude and expectations, and they misinterpreted what happened. It's easy to do in France.

The drive to the airport was uneventful. Saturday morning traffic was light enough that even I would have felt comfortable driving through it. We dropped the other two passengers off first. They had not wanted to fork over the additional two euros each, but did eventually, then skipped a tip, as anyone would who wasn't spineless. Our driver took us to the exterior Avis car drop-off area rather than to the interior rental counter, but it was close enough to where we needed to be that it wasn't a big deal. And it was certainly simpler than finding our way through the sprawling terminal, so it might have been worth the extra two euros, after all. I'd like to believe that, anyway.

Inside at the check-in counter, Micki was struck by how the workers, two young women, carried on an extended conversation between themselves (in French) as we waited for them to help us and then as they worked on our reservation. It seemed rude and inattentive, but they did get the job done. We checked in, declined the extra car insurance, and took our paperwork outside to the lady who earlier had directed us inside. She led us to our little Renault Clio diesel. As she walked around the champagne-colored car marking dings and scrapes on the official check-out diagram (so we wouldn't be charged for the extensive pre-existing damage), I began to think we *should* have sprung for the additional insurance, just to avoid any hassle if we would have a fender bender. I particularly felt that way when I discovered that the car was virtually brand-new, with only 8,000 miles on it.

We did not have an auspicious start to driving in France. Our first kilometer or two were used simply driving around the oval between terminals, a kind of service road connecting the various auto rental lots and looping around them. We couldn't tell where to leave it and ended up circling a few times before taking the plunge and shooting out into airport traffic. Little did we know how prophetic the experience would be.

Out of the car rental area, we were not much better off, because we still had no idea how to exit the sprawling airport. We drove around in circles, back and forth, crisscrossing the same territory multiple times, as well as discovering ever new ways to get lost. Eventually, we found a sign indicating a road to the nearby town of Roissy, and we took it. At least we should be able to locate ourselves on a map and figure out where we were going, then.

But the car rental company hadn't given us a map, not even a bad one (quite unlike my experiences renting a car in Germany, where my rentals *always* come with either a map or, in one case, an entire book of maps). What Avis *did* think essential enough to include with our car was a white plastic bag filled with French gossip magazines, the kind we might see in the checkout line of an American grocery store. We didn't bother looking at them or taking them with us, because we couldn't read them, didn't know the people in them, and didn't want to carry the extra weight with our luggage.

Fortunately, I had expected a bad map and brought my own photocopied map pages. All we had to do was locate ourselves on the page showing the airport. But, no, things weren't that simple. It seems that nothing is straightforward in France, and that includes the roads. Intending to head in to Roissy, we instead got entrapped in a series of roundabouts. The roads and all the roundabouts were all narrow and had no shoulder to pull over onto, so we couldn't stop and study the map together to get our bearings.

By the time we grew tired of guessing which exit to take and vowed to find our proper route, we were completely stymied. We stuck to one roundabout and drove in an everlasting circle, as slowly as we could without inciting the locals, squinting at each of the tiny road number signs we saw posted to see whether we could find any that matched up with where we should be, more or less.

"None of these numbers are on the map!" Micki wailed.

So we went around again, hoping to snag a different one. I turned into a bus stop lane, praying a loaded bus wouldn't pull up behind us, honking at us to move on. After a quick glance at the map and agreeing that none of the road numbers on it looked familiar, I pulled back into our circling pattern. Eventually I noticed that one of the signs had, in addition to road numbers, something marked *Coeur de France*, which, lo and behold!, was also written in italics along a road we wanted to take, so we finally had a direction to aim in.

But we were not home free. We still didn't know where we were or what road we were actually on. As far as we knew, we were heading *in the direction* of the Heart of France road, but still didn't know where it was or what else it might be called. And the road we were now on, as every other road we had been on so far and every road we would be on later, had no shoulder, no turnoff area, no place where we could just figure out what was going on.

I am, I must say, very good at reading maps and enjoy examining them just for the pleasure of it. However, I was the one driving, and we couldn't switch because of the manual transmission (which Micki couldn't drive), so I couldn't take a stab at locating us, and Micki was stuck trying to decipher the maps on her own. There's no denying that the French maps were a challenge for us, because all of the place names were unfamiliar, we didn't know how to pronounce most of them, and the road numbers on the maps didn't correspond with the numbers on the road signs. But we kept driving.

Finally, we stopped at an isolated rural gas station to get help. The workers spoke no English, but they figured out my butchered French and pulled out a Normandy map to show us where we were and how we were practically to Giverny—just follow the same road until we saw the signs for something we didn't hear but I assumed meant Claude Monet's house and gardens, then follow those, and they would take us through Giverny. I bought the voluminous map, as we would be spending the next couple of days in Normandy, and it might make sense to have a dedicated map of the region rather than the pages I had photocopied out of the fat Michelin map book I had for the entire country. Micki unfolded the new map in the car so she could track our progress.

"Jeez, Libby! This thing is like a blanket!"

It had taken over the passenger half of the car and covered Micki's lap, her front, her legs, and the gear shift. But it allowed her to keep track of where we were and where we needed to go, so we were grateful for it. We followed the driving instructions, and we drove right to Giverny, where we pulled into a parking lot and followed pedestrians up the hill and then right onto the street, directly to Monet's house and gardens.

There was a line to get in, of course, with it being August and high tourist season. While we waited to enter the house so we could buy our tickets, though, we were treated to the sight of a bride being photographed in front of the house—full white dress, white veil hanging down to her waist hiding her face, white-gloved hands clutching a bouquet of white flowers. After a few shots against the dense green shrubs, the bride and the photographer disappeared around Monet's house. Micki and I smiled. How wonderful for the young woman, to have her wedding photos taken in such a glorious setting!

Knowing we were on a fairly tight schedule, especially after wasting an hour or two leaving the airport and finding our route, we elected to see just the famous gardens and skip the house. And the gardens were *beautiful*, packed with blooms

Overgrown path in Monet's flower garden

overflowing their beds and crowding the various footpaths. It was an untidy profusion of plants, sections with pink and purple flowers, others with yellow and orange ones, an overall explosion of exuberant colors and delicate forms.

We crossed the street from Monet's backyard garden to his water garden, which we had recently seen in huge painted form at the Orangerie in Paris. While the Japanese bridge was there, and the drooping willows and the flowering lilypads, the colors were quite different from what I had expected based on the paintings I was familiar with. Instead of blues and purples, the actual site was filled with green, verdant green. I should have anticipated that. Monet famously liked to play with different lighting throughout the day, and obviously he had captured the dark colors at dusk, not high noon.

We tried to get good pictures of the water garden, but with all the other tourists trying to do the same, it was hard to get the scenery without either someone entering the frame holding up their own camera, or people posing for pictures at the best spots.

Bypassing the house on the way out, we headed back down the street we'd come in on. We talked constantly, admiring the houses as we passed them. The village was so pretty, bright with flowers, such a change from the sprawling farm country we were from, with its emphasis on production and practicality more than beauty. After, oh, maybe fifteen minutes of walking, it occurred to us that we should have passed our parking lot long before, and there was no sign of one anywhere near us. There were also no other tourists to be seen. We mentally reconstructed how we had approached Monet's house. (It was a little hazy, because all we'd done was follow a crowd of people from the car park.) We didn't come straight into this street, did we? No! We'd had to cut through a hedge and follow a street along the highway, then turn up the hill before walking on *this* street.

Monet's water garden

So we about-faced and walked, and walked, and walked back toward Monet's house, looking for anything familiar. We decided we must need to go back almost all the way to the museum to find the right cross street. As we neared that area of the village, we passed a hedge to the right, and at a break in the dense foliage, we could see there was a parking lot below. It wasn't where we had exited our lot, but we hoped to find our car there, and even if we couldn't, at least we would be down on the right level to walk around and look for it.

Fortunately, we spied our little Clio way to the back and the right, near the entrance from the highway, and no one had backed into it or banged doors into its sides. We opened the hot car up to air it out and pulled out our snack bags for a quick bite before driving again. We ate our granola bars and almonds, and Micki had one of the tiny packs of Twizzlers she had provisioned herself with for the trip. I so admired her restraint, to have two short little pieces of strawberry twist and be satisfied with that. She offered me some (as she always did), but I declined, because I knew I would want much more if I got started. I have a history with Twizzlers and know very well that starting on them is far easier than stopping.

Kind of the opposite of driving in France, where stopping is so much easier than starting. But we had a big chunk of Normandy to cross before the end of the day, so it was time to hit the road again.

12
A Norman Invasion

Our drive to the Normandy coast from Giverny would be primarily along expressways, the French version of our interstate highways. Although less picturesque than the Heart of France back-roads route, the expressways had the advantage of being far better marked and much easier to find, so we rolled onto the A13 with no problems. Soon after we joined the heavy traffic, however, it started to rain. Now, I know from painful experience *never* to leave a car rental parking lot without first locating where the headlights and the wiper controls are. However, in the confusion of getting our car that sunny morning and loading it up, I had completely forgotten to find the controls.

That important oversight never hit me until the rain did. The headlights were pretty easy to find. Also, I could pull forward on an arm on the steering column and get a sweep or two of the wipers. (I may well have been squirting wiper fluid at the same time—the windshield was too wet with rain to tell.) But for the life of me, I could not find the main wiper controls. So we hurtled down the interstate in the rain, with wipers sporadically cleaning the windshield for a second or two, dark skies continuing to rain down, all the while clawing and twisting at every protrusion we could find around the steering wheel and dashboard, trying to find the wiper controls. Traffic remained heavy, and—squinting at speeding cars through the blurry windshield, periodically whacking the intermittent wiper control—my tension level quickly spiked.

Fortunately, the rain stopped without any incident (also without us locating the wiper controls), but as the last drops fell, we joined a line of slowing traffic to go through our first toll booth. The various lanes were all marked for the type of payment they accepted. We drove below the sign that showed the silhouette of a person in a hat, hoping that meant we would be able to pay an attendant in cash there, and we felt a surge of victory when our hunch paid off.

Micki and I continued on the expressway, admiring the rolling green countryside now that the rain had stopped, and followed the same procedure when we came to a second toll booth. When we approached our third toll stop, however, between Rouen and Caen, traffic was horribly backed up, and we had to wait in a line that was miles long before we could pay and continue. Then, when we were free on the other side, we saw that cars were stacked up even farther from *that* direction, heading toward Paris.

We found out later from our hotelier that the traffic was that bad because so many people were traveling for the Feast of the Assumption, which was the next day. It is one of the Catholic church's most important holidays, honoring the Virgin Mary's assumption into heaven. France, of course, is a very Catholic country. Most French people might not see the inside of a church for the holy holiday, but they would celebrate it in their own way, which apparently required driving to somewhere *else* and overburdening the toll system.

We successfully found our way to the city of Bayeux, where

we would spend the night. I count it as remarkable that I was not honked at by a French driver until we reached a large roundabout at the edge of the city—that's how well we did with our driving (under *quite* difficult circumstances, I would note). And, really, regarding the honk, I thought I had left that guy in the roundabout *plenty* of space as I darted in, but apparently he didn't think so. Or maybe it was because I signaled to the *right* before turning right into all the roundabouts, and I noticed here that everyone else signaled to the *left* before turning right into the roundabouts, I suppose because they would be merging left into the traffic. You just never know which conventions will be different in a different country.

I knew our hotel was centrally located, near the famous tapestry and cathedral, so we just followed the city-center signs until we saw hotel signs. We found our hotel on the first drive by and even found a parking spot in the public parking area behind the building. As soon as I turned into the spot and sighed in relief that our day's drive was over, I declared that I was not going to drive again until we figured out how to run the windshield wipers.

We already knew from our earlier search that the glove box was empty. There was no manual in the car. So we investigated every nook and cranny of the driver's control area until I found where I could turn the wipers on and off. Finally! We would certainly need the wipers again, with all the wet weather that typically blows in from the nearby English Channel. After the fact, it was so obvious how to run the wipers that I couldn't believe we hadn't stumbled on the correct move with all the prodding and pulling we had done while racing along the expressway.

Grabbing our paperwork, we went in the back entrance to our hotel, talked to the friendly man running it—in English, no less—and learned that we could park right next to the building. We just needed to open up the chain barrier and drive in, which we did, so we would not have to haul our bags as far. The charming older man with his thin white hair checked us in and gestured to the side of the lobby by the door, where the wall was covered almost to the ceiling by a shallow wooden hutch filled with numbered pigeonholes. Topping each opening was a hook, many of them with keys dangling from them. The room keys, of course.

The man directed us to remove the key (and its two-pound brass holder) for room 8, and then indicated we should go one floor up to find our room. (In Paris, our hotel room had also been on the second floor. We were feeling pretty lucky, not having to climb to the upper reaches in our hotels.) It was obvious from the easily accessible rack of room keys which rooms were occupied and which were now empty. Apparently, the hotel staff was not as concerned about security as we were used to. Given the size and heft of the key tags, though, it was really not practical to take the key along when going out. (OK, the key tag wasn't really two pounds, but it *was* large and heavy, like having a tall jar of olives hanging from the key.)

We clunked with our suitcases up a flight of stairs, then turned down a hallway, followed it as it jogged once or twice, and then found our room. It was long and narrow, not large, but cheerful and nice. A three-star location. Our TV got several English stations—three versions of BBC, plus Sky News and CNN. Of course, we weren't in our room long enough to take advantage of them, but it's always a comforting touch of home to be able to hear the news in English.

Hanging our room key on a hook next to the others, we soon left the hotel to try to view the famous Bayeux Tapestry before the museum housing it closed. We rushed through the narrow street and around the corner, found the museum still open, paid our admittance fee and picked up our audio handsets with the explanations of what we would see. Eventually. First, though, we had to climb the stairs and wait for everyone before us to enter the dark room that displayed the famed needlework. When our time came, our handsets started and we got the history of the tapestry and some explication of what was depicted in the gory stitched scenes.

The Bayeux Tapestry was probably commissioned in the 1070s. It is an immense work of art—230 feet long—and shows the events that led up to the Norman conquest of England. Its fifty or so scenes include depictions of agricultural life at the time, Halley's comet (a bad omen), William the Conqueror arriving in England, and the 1066 Battle of Hastings—with bloody attacks and gruesome dismemberments and English King Harold apparently being killed with an arrow to his eye.

Although it would have been nice to linger and really examine the workmanship and the story depicted, we shuffled along in the dim light with all the other tourists, spurred to keep moving by the ongoing commentary. If we wanted to examine sections closely, we should have invested in some of the many tapestry items for sale in the gift shop or online, all adorned with copies of the embroidered scenes: mugs, t-shirts, mouse pads, pins, key chains, posters, cell phone covers, aprons, belt buckles, card decks, speakers, laptop skins, coasters, Christmas ornaments, jewelry, magnets, wall clocks, ties. Anything possible, it seemed, whatever the buyer might like. While some of the classier items were tempting—silk scarves, throw pillows—it would be dangerous to start collecting tapestry items, I would think, quickly growing expensive with fifty scenes to cover, if you wanted the whole story. And how could you have part of it—say, Harold visiting Bayeux—and not want the battle scenes and a bunch else, too?

We returned to the hotel to get advice from the white-haired gentleman at the desk about whether we needed to fill up the car before leaving town the next day, a Sunday. We decided we still had plenty of diesel to get us through the next day to Monday, since we weren't driving across half of France, or even across half of Normandy. The nice man did mark on a city map, though, where we could find a gas station (the only one?!) that would be open on Sunday.

We walked out again to view the outside of the nearby cathedral, Notre-Dame de Bayeux, because we thought we were too late to go inside. But, happily, the building was open and we could walk right in. We marveled at the Gothic architecture, the soaring limestone nave and colorful stained-glass windows.

The church was much older than its current Gothic form. It had played a part in the political dance between France and England before the Norman conquest. English King Harold (before he was king) supposedly vowed here not to challenge William of Normandy's claim to England. And when Harold broke that vow and did become king, William and his French army invaded England and conquered Harold and *his* army.

Bayeux's Notre-Dame Cathedral

*Soaring nave in the
Bayeux Cathedral*

It's all there in the Bayeux Tapestry, which originally—for hundreds of years—hung in this very cathedral.

Micki and I went down into the older Romanesque crypt, a fairly dark and musty place, but really quite clean for an ancient basement. We viewed the flaking 15th-century murals on the walls and pillars of the almost thousand-year-old crypt. Suddenly, we heard heavy organ music, somewhat muffled but a full-bodied accompaniment to our visit. It was traditional classical music, a rehearsal for a concert that would take place the next two nights, as we later saw in an announcement placed by the front door.

We followed the music back to the nave and sat on a hard and scarred wooden bench, listening. We caught all of Bach's "Toccata and Fugue" while we were there, as well as bits of other pieces. Magnificent! So moving, echoing through the practically empty interior of the massive stone building. After a rough day of driving, I almost cried. I wished we would be around for the next night's performance, but we would have moved on to Mont Saint-Michel by then.

We walked around the church to examine the exterior and saw an enormously huge tree that filled an entire square. I thought it must be a chestnut tree. As Micki can attest to, I tried to claim that every big tree I couldn't positively identify was a chestnut tree, but this one actually had prickly green chestnuts hanging on it. (After returning home, however, I discovered that the tree in question is a famous one, really a plane tree, with clusters of seed pods, not nuts, hanging off its branches. Such are my powers of horticultural identification.)

Suddenly we caught a whiff of divine aromas, of garlic, cheese, and baked crust, irresistibly drawing us onward. We were ravenous, having had only a light breakfast and then nothing at lunch other than a few snacks at our car in Giverny, so we headed to the nearby pizzeria for a late supper. The place was packed, but we found a small open table back in a corner. The overworked waitress was not able to tend to us immediately because of the crowd. I think she was the only one working the small dining room and the patio outside, and both were crammed full of hungry customers. We felt lucky to have found a table, though, and sat enjoying the warmth after being cold outside. Eventually, we were able to order, and pizza margherita with red wine made for a delicious supper.

This was the first time Micki had had Italian-style pizza, thin and crispy, baked in a wood oven, where each person has his or her own pie. She was skeptical about the serving size and wondered whether we should split one. I resisted, assuring her that most people really do eat their own pizza, and as hungry as I was, I greedily wanted my own. She had a ham, cheese, mushroom version, which I admit looked even better than my margherita (cheese, tomato sauce, and basil). About

Gargoyle downspout on the cathedral in Bayeux

halfway through mine, I thought maybe she had been right and we should have split one, but we both finished ours, and we were gloriously full afterwards.

Happily sated, we continued our walk around the cathedral to the front again, hoping we would see it illuminated for the night, but it was still too light out for that on this late summer evening, even though it was after nine. So we ambled back toward the hotel, detouring to follow a bit of the picturesque river walk, where we saw an old mill with a water wheel churning next to a dam. An evocative spotlight highlighted the wooden wheel and the surrounding planters bursting with pink, purple, and white flowers. The scene reminded me of Marie Antoinette's hamlet at Versailles. Bayeux was such a pretty town, with all the yellow stone buildings and flower boxes spilling over with blooms.

Back at the hotel, I checked out a netbook for Internet use and sat in the breakfast room with other travelers who were talking, drinking wine, or also on the Internet. I checked my email and quickly updated my Facebook status.

Successfully drove to Normandy today, after circling endlessly to get the right roads (LOVE those roundabouts!), visiting Monet's gardens, and getting stuck in holiday traffic. Saw the Bayeux Tapestry and the gorgeous cathedral here. Everything is so beautiful. If a bit cool....

I discovered later that night, while looking through the little brochure of hotel information, that the Internet computer cost was five euros for a half hour. Yikes! How long had I been online?? The extra expense niggled at the back of my mind, because I was sure I could have been faster if I'd realized that time was costing me. I do hate wasting money.

Back in the room, I called home. The second phone card we had picked up in Paris was working great. As far as I could tell, when we called directly from our room, we still

Old mill along the river in Bayeux

had something like 9,000 "units" left, which seemed insane, but I was sure the lady on the recording kept saying *neuf mille*. It was a wonderful touch of home to hear the kids and John. This was the night I would miss my stepfather's 55th birthday party, which was unfortunate. I was making a habit of that; I had also missed his 50th birthday when I was in Montréal with my mother, to see what the French language and culture were like in Québec.

After phone calls, we were ready to call it a night. It had been a long and difficult day, and we knew we had another full day of sights and driving before us. So we showered and, hoping for a good night's sleep before the next day's challenges, slipped gratefully between crisp white sheets.

13
American Heroes

Micki and I awoke to a steady rain the next morning. Up at seven, we were happy that the bathroom in this hotel was larger than the one we had had in Paris—we could actually haul our full backpacks in and not have to pull out the three or four separate bags that contained our normal prep materials.

We were downstairs for breakfast by eight, two of only a handful who were up and about that early. The breakfast was probably overpriced at ten euros, but it was tasty and convenient. What else would be open on a Sunday morning—Assumption Day, no less—in the center of an old village? Our euros bought us orange juice, a hot drink (tea for me, *chocolat* for Micki), and a bread basket with a croissant, partial baguette, and a chocolate chip flaky rectangular thing for each of us.

We also had access to the buffet of boiled eggs, ham and cheese, fruit cocktail, applesauce, corn flakes, muesli, milk, plain yogurt, dried apricots, raisins, jams, butter, honey, and Laughing Cow cheese spread. Canned fruit cocktail is an ever popular breakfast item in France, which is a mystery to me. Does anyone actually *like* fruit cocktail? When I was growing up that was always the last can of fruit left in the cupboard. No one ate fruit cocktail. Once in a while, I buy a can myself—for more variety among the canned fruits in our cupboard, or perhaps just out of tradition—but we never eat it, either. It gathers dust until the next Boy Scout food drive, and then out it goes with the pumpkin pie filling I didn't use at Thanksgiving. Peaches, pears, pineapple—all those canned versions appeal more than fruit cocktail. Yet, I think the mushy mixed fruit has appeared at most hotel breakfasts I have seen in France. The French are, indeed, a mysterious people.

Micki and I loaded up on enough fuel to last us through the day. We knew it wasn't an authentic French way to break-fast (more than coffee and a light pastry), but the food was there and we'd paid a lot for it, plus we had no lunch plans. So, better safe than sorry, and hand me another plate of cheese, please.

I was pleasantly surprised when we paid our hotel bill to see that we had not been charged for using the Internet or the phone. Our fondness for the charming hotel and its delightful owner was growing by the minute, and we regretted that we couldn't stay longer than one night before moving on.

We packed up our car, checking the wiper controls to make sure we remembered where they were. Then off we headed for the D-Day sites, which took no time at all to reach, since we were already so close to the coast. Of course, after parking in a pay lot and wandering around for a few minutes, we dis-covered that we had driven to the wrong place—*in* the town of Arromanches instead of *above* Arromanches. But as long as we were there, we checked out the remains of Port Winston, the name given to the temporary harbor that the Allies cre-ated to unload troops and supplies after the D-Day invasion. Pontoons and sections of steel roadways had been towed by tug boats across the channel and then assembled to form a flexible, floating dock where ships could unload safely regardless of the changing water levels from the tides. The idea for the artificial harbor had come from Winston Churchill himself (hence, the nickname Port Winston) and is thought to be one of the greatest feats of military engineering ever.

Standing above the beach, we didn't investigate the visible remains more closely because of the unpleasant weather and not wanting to get our sandals all dirty in the wet sand. We returned to the car and drove out of town, or, more accurately, we drove through the town a few times, circling around the one-way loop of the town center, trying to find which way to go. At least we were able to work the wipers this day and could keep our windshield clear. We saw some signs to what we thought was our goal—Operation Overlord—and headed off where they indicated. We traveled quite a bit on the narrow, winding road before deciding that we were driving the wrong way, *completely* the wrong way. We were traveling west but needed to be *east* of town if we were going to find the Arromanches 360 museum that would give us the overview we wanted before visiting other sites.

We managed to get turned around despite the lack of convenient drives or parking lots. Fortunately, traffic was sparse, and I was able to execute a three-point turn on the narrow road. Back we drove to Arromanches, and after a few more loops around the center, with more squinting at signs through the rain, we tootled off in the right direction and found the 360-degree film we had been looking for. *The Price of Liberty* provided D-Day footage projected in a full circle around us, on nine huge screens, intermixed with modern shots of the battlefields. It was a good film, but it hurt my ears with all the artillery fire. We could *feel* the noise of the blasts. It was certainly loud enough that extended exposure would cause hearing damage, and I'm sure the real experience was much worse. The old men I knew who had served in WWII all had terrible hearing, and even with their hearing aids, it was hard to converse with them. Here was ample evidence why. Because the theater building was on a bluff overlooking the city of Arromanches, we also had a view over Port Winston. We stood on the overlook, battling the winds and rain with our straining umbrellas, and when the discomfort became too great, we immediately sought shelter in our car. We realized how fortunate we were to have that option. We endured the elements at our pleasure, then holed up warm and snug and safe in our reliable modern vehicle. What a different experience than that of the troops on that long-ago rainy day! They had no escape from the unpleasant weather, which must have compounded the misery of the attack.

Next we drove west of town (again) and passed through the quaintest village down the coast (again), where a limestone house was built so close to the road that a corner jutted practically into the road itself. How could it not be clipped by passing trucks or campers? Yet, it looked intact. Flowerboxes provided the only bright spots in the steady drizzle, but the drive was not unattractive. The route already felt familiar from our earlier visit. We headed for Omaha Beach and the visitor center at the American cemetery and, miraculously, found our way with no difficulty.

Inside the visitor center, we saw a small crowd gathering at the start of the exhibit, near the entrance to a theater. A group soon exited through the doors, and we entered the dim, hushed room and seated ourselves about halfway back, not sure what we would encounter after the booming violence of the 360-degree film we had just seen. This film was different, though, and rather than providing an overview of the main events, it zoomed in to the personal, sharing the history and fates of a handful of individuals, not famous heroes, just average Joes. I was struck by their youth, by their dutifulness, by their bravery and too-often tragic stories. I found myself fighting back tears, trying to wipe my eyes without anyone seeing and wishing we'd sat in the back, where my furtive swipes would not be visible to all behind us. My sniffs and discreet nose-blowing would have been hard to hide anywhere, though. I hate it that I get so emotional.

Those tears surfaced easily throughout the day as we walked slowly through the museum, reading displays, watching videos. We read of the incredible dangers faced and heroics performed by the troops. The excellent information told how the Americans were supposed to invade a day earlier than they did, that they had deployed on that schedule, but the weather was so bad and the seas so rough that they were stuck on the landing craft *on* those rough seas overnight before the invasion could go forward a day later.

I can get motion sick on an elevator and imagined all too well how dreadfully seasick and miserable those poor boys must have been with the storm swells up to five or six feet. All day, all night, pitching them about. And I can't help calling them boys. They were so young—18, 19?—and looked like the young, young men that they were. After spending the night bobbing on heavy seas in the biting wind and the rain, battered by the elements, they had to muster the energy and spirit to jump off those boats into cold water up to their waists or chests or necks, waves beating against them as they held their guns aloft to keep them dry and functioning.

They dodged the barriers set by the Nazis—the mines, the concertina wire—and hid behind spindly anti-tank hedgehogs for what cover they could find, hoping they wouldn't get shot by the gunners who trained machine guns on them from the bluffs above. Britain's D-Day Museum in Portsmouth reports that D-Day resulted in 2,499 American fatalities, out of 4,413 Allied fatalities (attributed to research by the U.S. National D-Day Memorial Foundation). The dead from that dreadful day numbered well more than three times the entire population of my hometown. *Three times.* On one day. Exposure to the elements alone would have been enough to bring me down. Where did those men find the strength, the courage to push onward in the face of those obstacles and unspeakable dangers?

Before the exit of the visitor center—I think it was the final display—a simple scene behind glass took my breath away and started the waterworks again. A rifle, its bayonet stuck into a sea of white rocks, stood with a dark green helmet placed over the top, curved over the butt of the gun like an empty turtle shell. We've all seen this image before, honoring dead servicemen, but there were so, so many dead at D-Day.

A sober reminder of the fallen at D-Day

08/15/2010

The American Cemetery at Omaha Beach

In the cemetery, rows of white crosses stretched as far as the eye could see. The well-kept green grass contrasted pleasingly with the white marble markers. The cemetery is a piece of the United States, given to our country by the grateful French government. We stood in the cold rain, looking at the cold stone markers, at the names, the too-young ages, the home states. Too many markers were for unidentified bodies and lacked any personal information, saying instead, "Here rests in honored glory a comrade in arms known but to God." A dignified marker, an honorable end, but what a loss for loved ones, not only missing their son, their brother, their husband, but not knowing where he lay, or even whether he had fallen during the fighting at all. How long had those families hoped in vain before they learned the truth, or as much of the truth as anyone was able to tell them? The uncertainty must have been torturous, the final loss devastating.

Most of the grave markers were standard crosses, but

the Star of David was well represented. By the time of D-Day, Jewish soldiers must have known of the atrocities being perpetrated against their fellow Jews. Maybe that, in part, was where the remarkable bravery of the servicemen came from—from the knowledge that they represented a force for good, beating back an unspeakably evil madman. Below us, the frigid waves slapped against the sand, a reminder of what those gallant, dead heroes had slogged through. Wave after wave broke over the beach, just as wave after wave of men had marched ashore or fallen in the attempt.

We wandered to the long, semi-circular Wall of the Missing, panel after panel inscribed with identifying information. Small metal rosettes marked the names of those whose bodies had since been recovered and identified, but they were very much in the minority. Most of the missing remained missing, and they must have represented every state.

*PATTERSON RICHARD L * S SGT * 300 ENGR COMBAT BN * IOWA*

*PAULS ELWOOD G * TEC 5 * 262 INF 66 DIV * SOUTH DAKOTA*

Pennsylvania. Texas. Ohio. Connecticut. Minnesota. Massachusetts. California. New York. Wisconsin. Indiana. Florida. Mississippi. North Carolina. The list went on, 1,557 names in all.

A large outdoor map of the D-Day battle plan displayed red arrows as if in an elaborately choreographed dance—a twisted, deadly Arthur Murray guide—showing the various attacks and movements of the Allied troops. The complexity was mind-boggling. I can only marvel at what was accomplished, and how it was accomplished, and feel unutterably grateful that we have not seen the likes of that destruction

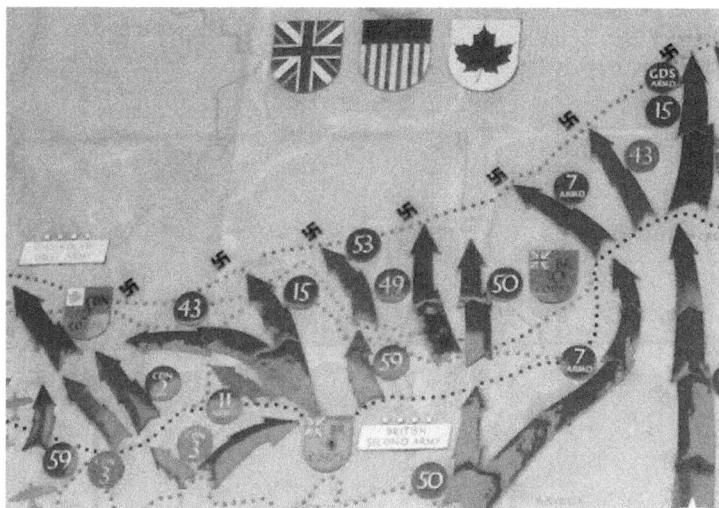

A small portion of the plans for the D-Day invasion

again, not to the same devastating extent and depth.

We left the site sober but glad we had visited it, glad we had paid our respects and seen just a glimpse of what that dreadful day might have been like. I wished that I had my family with me, so they could experience it and learn from it. I wished I had traveled to the old battlefields with Gerald, my grandmother's old beau who had battled in the war and was now gone. I wished I had encouraged him to talk more about it and openly honored his service more.

I write this chapter just days before Veterans' Day, and my eyes are filled with tears of thanks and sadness. So much was lost on D-Day; so much was saved. I am not alone in my gratitude. I had read that the French people of Normandy are grateful to this day for the Americans and what they did to free France. Micki and I did not stay long in that part of the country, but we felt very welcome while we were there. We met with nothing but friendliness and helpfulness in the people we spoke with, and we encountered more English language than we would anywhere else we visited in France. Our visit to Normandy was somber, it was cold, windy and wet, but we would both eagerly return, if the opportunity arose.

14
Beyond Land's End

We left Omaha Beach at 1:45, deciding to skip the stop at the nearby German gun battery. Instead we drove directly to Mont Saint-Michel, which we found after only moderate panic and confusion. We had a little trouble finding our right roads (or realizing we were *on* our right roads), and it rained almost constantly until shortly before our arrival on the Mont. Fortunately, we had filled up before leaving Bayeux, so we didn't have to worry about our fuel situation, and that little Renault Clio seemed to sip the diesel, anyway.

We probably didn't need a full tank for our modest drive of the day, but we didn't want to risk running low on diesel in unfamiliar territory. The nice older man from our hotel had kindly told us which gas station was the only one open on Sunday *with an attendant*. We would need to pay an actual human, because our American credit cards did not contain the chip-and-PIN technology that most French self-pay machines require for security reasons. The man had marked the spot on a city map for us, and it was even easy to find, with virtually no traffic to contend with on a Sunday morning.

At the pump, I triple- or quadruple-checked to make sure I was putting in the right fuel, but the car rental company had wisely placed a sticker right next to the gas tank labeled "Diesel/Gazoil" so I couldn't really screw it up. We also used the bathroom at the gas station. I had some trouble getting the toilet to flush, because the button on top wouldn't push in. After a minute or two of fruitless pokes and twists at the button on the tank, I finally thought to *pull up* on the small knob, and the tank immediately emptied. We had encountered many dual-flush push options already, but that was the first (and only) pull-up knob we saw.

After the D-Day sites, we drove narrow, winding roads in the rain, with oncoming cars blasting by uncomfortably close to the driver's side of our car. Veering slightly to the right, I once drove *just* off the asphalt, where the right wheels dropped down several inches to the mud, and the car jerked wildly off the road, like it was possessed. There was no problem getting back onto the road, but when I deliberately pulled off a couple of times later to consult our map, I was very careful because of the jarring drop and strong pull to the side.

Eventually, we entered the expressway and enjoyed its wider lanes and better signs, even if we didn't appreciate the faster pace and heavier traffic. It was still the holiday weekend, after all, and it appeared that half of France was heading to the northern coast for their vacation. With relief, we saw the road signs indicating the exit for Mont Saint-Michel. After leaving the expressway, we joined the long line of campers and busses on the two-lane road that wound the last miles to the shore. Ahead of us, rising in the distance, was the rugged silhouette of the famous abbey drawing us onward, its towering spire puncturing the sky atop the looming structure, high on the rocky island.

At last we turned right onto the coastal road, drove past the fields of campers and RVs, and then left onto the causeway

The island of Mont St-Michel

that led us 600 meters (almost 2,000 feet) through the bay
and out to the island itself. The rain that had dogged us all
day was gone and would stay away the whole time we were
on the Mont. Because we were staying overnight on the island, we were directed to a parking lot below the causeway
road. That worried me a bit, because I had read stories of
cars floating away from the lower levels at times of high tide.
I didn't quite trust the five-language sign assuring us that
"Today the sea does not cover this carpark." I would rather
have parked on the upper level at the side of the road, just to
be sure we wouldn't lose the car to the sea in the night. But
we had no choice, so I nosed the car down the embankment
to the lower lot.

No one is likely to lose their car to the tides there in the
future. The raised causeway was constructed in 1879 and
over the years has contributed to the silting up of the bay by
cutting off natural water movement. A new elevated bridge
has been built since Micki and I were there, to connect the

Parking sign at Mont St-Michel

island to the mainland, and the artificial causeway and parking lots will eventually be removed. That will allow water from the tides and the Couesnon River that empties there to clean out the silt and surround the island with water again. Parking will then be on the mainland. If Micki and I return, we will need to either walk across the bridge to the island or ride a shuttle bus.

This day, though, we parked outside the fortress walls. We hauled our suitcases behind us, up the stairs from the parking lot to the road, down the other side of the road, along a boardwalk to the entrance through the protective wall that fortified the town, and then into a sort of courtyard, where guards formerly would have stood. A heavy iron grate still hung at the top of a second gate, looking as if it could clang down and close off the opening to the island at any time, possibly impaling us with the spikes along its bottom edge.

We entered the main (and only) street of the village. The narrow lane was packed with tourists from around the world. We heard a babel of languages—Italian, Spanish, German, British English—but very few of the voices were American. By the time of our late afternoon arrival, more tourists were wandering downhill toward the exit gate than were entering the fortress, so we were bucking the flow with our luggage. The crowded street was lined with souvenir shops, restaurants, a few hotels. It was a sensory overload. What with the

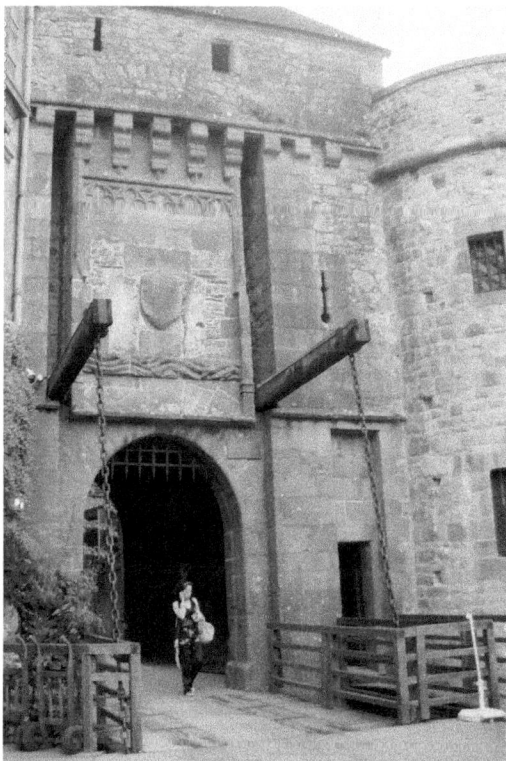

Drawbridge and inner gate at Mont St-Michel

moving masses of people, with the many signs both on the buildings and sticking out above them, with trying not to bump people as we shouldered through the throng with our backpacks and rolling suitcases, we were not able to find a sign for our hotel. At one point, we stopped and turned to look back, trying a new perspective.

Micki pointed down the hill to the left. "Isn't that our hotel?"

It was hard to see, but there it was, a sign next to the lamb restaurant. We entered the ground floor and discovered we should go up one flight to the hotel reception, where the keys were. We were checked in, then led up another narrow flight of stairs, through some French doors and right across the middle of a restaurant dining room, our suitcase wheels

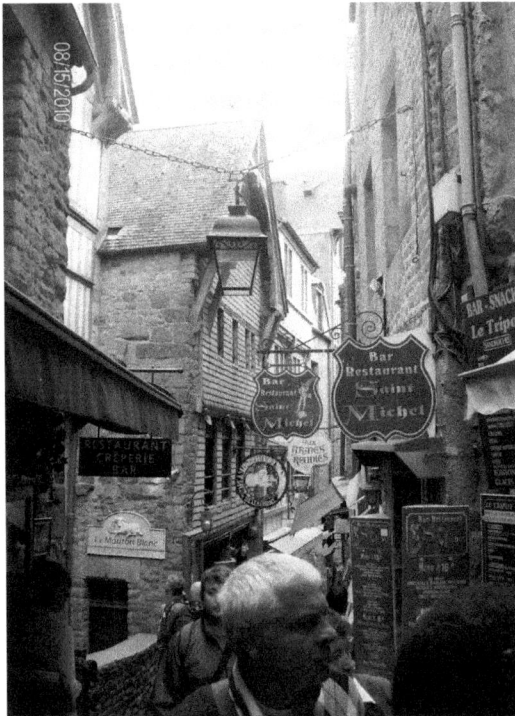

Main street on Mont St-Michel

humming on the hardwood floor. Fortunately, the room was empty at this time of day, and we didn't interrupt anyone's dinner. Then out we went onto the ramparts (the elevated walkway between the buildings and the city walls, where archers could defend against invaders). We bumped our suitcases along the ramparts a bit, then our guide stopped at a narrow bi-fold door (really narrow, with just one fold), then went up a staircase so steep and narrow that we had to turn our small suitcases sideways to accommodate them. Our room was one of two up there in the "Atelier."

After unloading our luggage, we reentered the human stream on the street and continued our climb to the abbey at the top of the twisting lane. Our steps slowed and our breath quickened as we marched higher, higher, higher. We reached a bend, a turn where the route headed farther up and inland, and we took advantage of the spot to admire the view over the wall and to catch our breath. But then we were onward and upward again, hauling our bodies, heaving them up each step as we neared the end of the climb. The outer walls and gates of the church were in view.

When we completed the climb and entered the St. Michael's abbey complex, I was winded but amused by the prominently displayed emergency defibrillator on the wall. How often were cardiac events triggered by the immense vertical effort to reach the church? How did authorities evacuate patients to the hospital? We were at the top of a remote medieval pilgrimage site. The street on the island was too narrow, uneven and twisting for an ambulance. The roads through the mainland village and along the coastline were clogged with tourists. Where even *was* the nearest hospital? Did the authorities call in a medical helicopter, in the case of a medical emergency, or did they just let the poor sufferer expire there at the base of the shrine to St. Michael? I felt on the verge of expiring, myself, and realized—if I hadn't already—that

I need to see such hard-to-access sights while still relatively young and healthy.

We were standing in the "Marvel," where the Archangel Michael had reportedly appeared to a local bishop in 708 and told him to build a church on the site. The part of the legend I really like (unfortunately not verified) is that, when the bishop kept ignoring the demand to build, Michael took his finger and burned a hole into the bishop's skull. Apparently that finally got his attention, and the first monastery went up. It has served as a pilgrimage site ever since and has been modified, rebuilt, and added to over the years. I thought the Mont was hard for *us* to access, that *we* were now beyond the reaches of the modern world. But what about the pilgrims who walked untold distances to get there, to that remote corner of France, out on an island, surrounded by either quicksand or pounding tides? I'd like to imagine that at the end of their journey, the pilgrims climbed the rough stone stairs, rising endlessly up to and next to the abbey, on their knees, to really complete the picture of devout suffering. I was not physically fit, however, and just trudging up the incline was suffering enough for me.

We took a self-guided tour of the abbey from a guidebook, which was a wonderful wander through the labyrinth of the former monastery. It pleased me to see the sign on the wall marking the eating hall (the refectory), in French, announcing that it was "des moines," of the monks. Being from Iowa, I was well familiar with the name Des Moines and even lived in our state capital for several years. However, I had no idea that the city name had anything to do with monks. As far as I had known, it was just derived from the Fort Des Moines that had once stood there, after the name given to the site by earlier French trappers. I vowed to investigate what the name meant in the context of the city of Des Moines, but forgot about it by the time of my return. (A later search revealed that the settlement was likely named after the Des Moines River, which had—likely—been named after a group of Trappist monks who lived in huts at the river's mouth. Either that, or it was named after a Miami-Illinois chief's insulting name for a competing tribe—Moingoana—which according to a March 23, 2007, *Des Moines Register* article, means "the excrement-faces." I'm going with the monk version.)

During an outdoor section of our wander—on a walled terrace overlooking the salty mud flats—we could see a tour group far below us, wearing their rain coats and high rubber boots as they were guided safely across the treacherous sands. I regarded the sands stretching into the distance with respect. They could suck down the unwary with their submerged water currents, commonly known as quicksand. They could be

Human "hamster wheel" in the abbey, formerly used to haul goods up the steep hill

covered in quick order by tides that are the highest in Europe (32-52 feet) and among the fastest and strongest in the world, "as fast as a galloping horse," up to 12 mph when conditions are right. The flats were open to quickly rolling storms from the English Channel, putting any humans on the sands in great danger from lightning, because there's nothing around taller than they are. I was in no hurry to walk the sandy mud flats of the bay.

We ate at the lamb restaurant next door to our hotel, and both of us had the "menu" for 22 euros. We should have ordered lamb, because the area is renowned for its unique salt-flavored mutton, from the flocks grazing on salt-infused

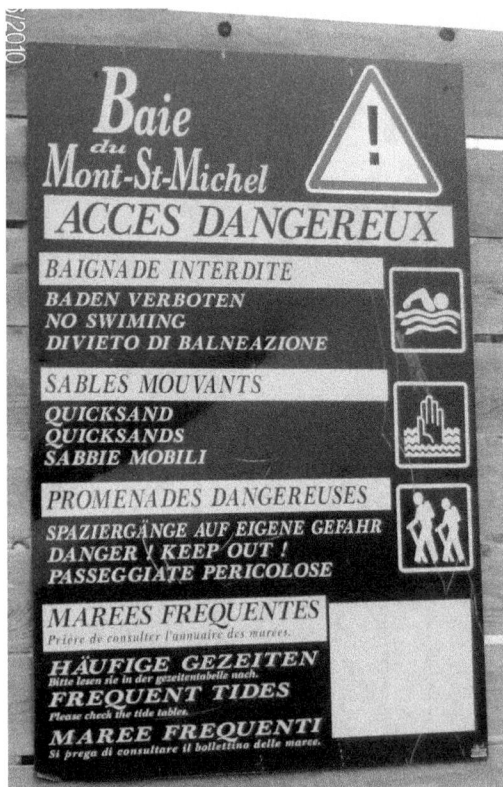

Sign warning of dangers in the Bay of Mont St-Michel

grasses along the coast. But we ordered steak. I thought our waiter looked like Steve Carell in black-rimmed glasses, but Micki wasn't convinced. He was nice enough, at any rate, and tolerated my weak French, as English didn't seem to be an option. I ordered my steak well-done (given the French fondness for undercooking), which turned out to be a mistake.

The waiter had really tried to get me to order medium, which Micki did, but I didn't want any bloodiness, so I stuck with well-done. That usually would have brought me a nicely cooked medium in France, but something went wrong. Micki's steak was a perfect medium-rare, and mine was way *over*done, like shoe leather, almost uneatable, so maybe medium is the way to go. Personally, I wondered whether the chef was punishing me for ordering my meat "overcooked" by French standards to begin with. I probably should have sent it back as barely edible, but for all I know, that's how that guy interpreted well-done, and the waiter knew it, which was why he had tried to get me to change.

Micki and I shared a famous "puffy omelette" that supposedly originated at a different restaurant on the island and is its signature dish, but neither of us cared for it. For one thing, the whipped white was partially runny, which I really dislike. We also split the goat cheese/cured ham appetizer. I still don't care for cured ham; it's just too *raw* for me. We don't really eat raw meat where we're from. Everything was presented beautifully, though. We had French fries with the steak, wine with the meal, and apple tart for dessert. We were stuffed. It was a wonderful feeling, after not eating since breakfast.

We noticed at supper how empty the restaurant was—just us and, eventually, a couple with two children—and how bored our waiter appeared, returning to the door to look out, as if he could *will* people to arrive. I expect that the restaurant had been packed during the day, when the whole island was crammed with visitors, but it was deserted at night.

Lamb restaurant next to our hotel

Our hotel was... interesting. The building was very old (as, I suppose, everything is on the ancient *mont*), with the bathroom carved out of our room, spoiling its original shape. This is, of course, one reason that the hotel bathrooms across France are usually as small as they are—the space is stolen from pre-existing and usually very old rooms. Look at a bedroom in your house and imagine enclosing a bathroom in one of its corners—that's what French hoteliers were looking at, once tourists started demanding private bathrooms rather than being willing to share one down the hall. And I'm part of the problem, I admit. As I've grown older and more used to a private bath, that's one of my requirements in searching for accommodations on a trip.

This room was not only oddly shaped, but the walls were a faded Pepto-Bismol pink. We had two windows in the bedroom—one looking out over the ramparts to the mud flats, and one on the side overlooking the terrace of the crêperie next door, which also let us look out over the flats of the bay. In the bathroom we had another large window, which did not have any curtains on it, or any shades or blinds of any sort. That wasn't a problem during the day—we were high enough up that no one could see us—but I was quite uncomfortable at night, not really knowing whether people were able to see in or not. It was especially uncomfortable with so little space in the bathroom. There wasn't room to dry oneself after a shower over *by* the shower, which left the cramped area in front of the window. Really, it was definitely snug in there— we actually had to climb over the toilet to get to the shower. I waited and cleaned up the next morning, when I didn't worry about people being able to see in. I would have felt completely exposed drying in front of that naked window, a black blank into the night, even if no one would have been able to see in. Micki was brave and showered at night, brushing off my concerns.

"I don't know anyone and would never see them again, anyway."

"You'll probably get your picture taken, now that every phone has a camera. If you end up on YouTube, it's not MY fault!" I hate the loss of privacy that's come with all those stupid phone cameras….

Apparently, no one at our hotel spoke English, so I had to dig up my rudimentary French anytime I needed to communicate. I knew it would come in handy off the beaten path, and it doesn't get much more off the beaten path than Mont Saint-Michel.

We wanted to check in with our families in the evening and let them know we had arrived safely, but had to use a public telephone in the main building, in a hallway next to the restaurant, even though we had a phone in our room. We had tried to call from there, but there were too many "implosions" involved, and we couldn't. We had no idea what those mysterious implosions were, but they had something to do with the units required to place a call and the units remaining on our phone card, and we did not have a good mix to call from our private phone. As no one in our hotel spoke English, we couldn't ask for an explanation, but they were able to tell us to use the phone in the hall. And, for some reason, when we used our phone card on the French Telecom public phone, all of a sudden, we only had 90 minutes of call time for the U.S. Clearly, our credits went much farther on private lines, where it looked like we were being charged for a local call, even when our calls were overseas.

I had been experiencing hip, back, and thigh pain for several days. Sometime in our rambles through Paris—and I *know* while we were at Versailles—I had stumbled enough on the many uneven surfaces that my hip was killing me. It must have been pretty early in our trip, because I know stairs had bothered me by the time we went up the Arc de Triomphe, which was our second day in France. So maybe the flight or hauling luggage was the original culprit. (Or maybe the stairs at Ste-Chapelle, with their trebuchet warning sign!)

At any rate, the situation was not improving, and I was not only out of breath mounting long stretches of stairs, but I was in pain. There wasn't an even walking surface on the whole island of Mont Saint-Michel—everything was up steps or down steps or along uneven cobblestones or even larger and even more irregular stones. So that evening, I lay down on the floor of our pink room (taking up approximately half the available floor space) and braced my right leg against the bathroom wall, so I could give myself a hip adjustment, which I had learned to do several years before during physical therapy.

Micki kindly made no comment as I pushed and went through my adjustment routine, but it wouldn't have fazed me if she had. When I can tell something has been jolted out of place and every step results in a cry and semi-collapse, I will lie down next to the nearest suitable wall to get things back in working order, and I don't care who thinks I'm crazy. I once flopped onto the floor of Chicago's crowded Museum of Science and Industry and let other visitors walk around me, because I was in such pain and needed to adjust my hip joint. And, while relief isn't immediate, by the next day, I'm back to normal.

After we had dinner in the restaurant that night, Micki and I went back down to the parking area to take evening shots of the island. We were amazed by how few people were around, once the day-trippers had left. Down at lower levels, we could see the Mont with lights shining on it, even though it wasn't dark yet. It looked magnificent, and I took loads of pictures, knowing that most of them would be blurry in the fading light. My very last picture, where I steadied my camera on the post of a traffic barricade, actually turned out well, so I do have one good one. The one right before that would have been good, too, but a woman bumped the barrier when I was taking the shot, which made my camera jiggle. She apologized, but it was not a big deal, thanks to digital photography and the opportunity to take as many shots as I wanted. When Micki and I left to go back up to the walled village, that woman and the man she was with quickly took my spot to try their own picture.

After entering the gate into the walls again, we saw a narrow flight of stairs heading, it looked, up to the *left* side of the church. We had not been there yet, so we started climbing, even though it was getting dark. For some time, there had been an absolute cacophony in one of the trees in the middle of the bluff, behind the buildings along the main street. Micki had wondered whether the birds making all the noise might be bats, but we decided that bats didn't congregate in trees like that. Maybe they were sparrows, since we had seen masses of sparrows on the island. But the cawing tree was quite a way off to our right as we climbed the new set of stairs, so we gave up our guesswork. We turned on a landing, and then headed farther up toward what looked like a little garden. We never made it all the way, though, because suddenly, a black shape came zigzagging right at my head. I ducked and went into panic mode.

"Bats!" I shrieked to Micki, cowering and covering my head with my arms. We turned and practically tumbled down the stairs in our mad dash to get back to the entrance courtyard by the fortress wall, then we scampered up another set of stairs to the ramparts that led to our hotel. We scurried along the ramparts toward our room to enjoy what was left of a view from there inside, safe from flying vermin.

The views, of course, were of the vast sand flats. It should have been high tide then, but the bay looked nothing like pictures I had sighed over before our trip. Instead of dramatically smashing waves that sent white foam crashing up the sides of the Mont, we saw only a weenie-looking stream. Apparently the tide is only *really* high at new and full moons, which we were missing. The only tide we saw was a trickle of water slowly flowing landward through the flats in the evening, and then slowly flowing seaward in the morning. The mud flats were by no means as grand to look at as stormy seas would have been, so that was a disappointment, but they were definitely interesting and otherworldly. And we didn't need to worry about our car floating away, so the lower tide had that going for it.

I couldn't help wondering throughout our stay what it was like to live on Mont Saint-Michel, so remote and separate. The traditional livelihood was the pilgrimage business—tourism, same as today—so people stayed busy, but what beyond that? How isolated was life? I suppose people were adept at reading the tides and knowing when it was safe to cross the sand

City wall on Mont St-Michel, with sand flats in the background

(before the days of the causeway). There must have been brisk trade and traffic between the island and the mainland. After all, *someone* had to deliver all the food, building supplies, and everything else needed to keep life running offshore. But, still, what was it like living there before easy transportation? Before the Internet? Before satellite television? Before telephones?? These questions really applied to any isolated location, but the physical separation of the Mont from the mainland emphasized its stark loneliness.

That is part of its appeal, of course. The "Marvel" is a piece of ancient past, and with its remoteness, its craggy structures and inaccessibility, it seems to transport us to a different age, to a time of battlements and saintly sightings, of sieges and pilgrims. Realistically, Mont Saint-Michel may not be a great place to live, but Micki and I loved visiting it.

Except for the bats.

15
The Terrible Ts

We had a bad night's sleep on Mont Saint-Michel, in our odd pink room high above the fortress walls. After the sun set, it was pitch black out, with no lights on our side of the island over the sandy mud flats to the sea. Sleep should have come easily, but instead *it* started. Something, somewhere, made noise through the night. *Wham!* Silence. *Slam!* Silence. A shutter banging in the wind? Someone breaking through the flimsy folding door at the bottom of our stairs? Ghosts?? We were so isolated that if anyone had tried to break in, no one would have heard our cries of alarm. That knowledge didn't help me nod off. Whatever the noise was, it was spooky and loud enough to startle me out of sleep anytime I drifted off.

In the morning, both of us were slightly groggy from the noisy night. Micki had the brilliant idea of taking our suitcases to the car before breakfast, so we wouldn't have to haul as much all at once and battle our way through the influx of day-tripping tourists. We were able to wrestle our cases around the bed, out the door to the cramped landing, sideways down the narrow steps, and through the tiny bi-fold door at the bottom of the stairs, then along the ramparts and down the uneven stone stairs to the cobblestone street, out through the thick city wall, across the elevated causeway to the parking area to our car. Really, it was that simple!

And it worked great. We had a clear shot out to the car without thousands of tourists buffeting us on their way in. (As we had spent the *night* on the island, I felt morally superior to those who just flitted in for a few hours. Had *they* braved the bats and the midnight ghosts of martyrs past? No!) We were soon back for breakfast. Baguette, croissant, two slices of toast, butter, jam and honey, applesauce, orange juice, and hot drink—nine euros per person. (But where was the fruit cocktail??) Then we loaded up the rest of our baggage and successfully drove our route for the day under clear skies and with little traffic.

That was the good part.

Almost immediately after we left the island, we had to contend with the toilets *en route*, or, rather, the lack of them. That morning for breakfast, as with most hotel breakfasts, we each got an individual drink: Micki had a little pot of cocoa, and I had a cute pot of tea, enough for at least two piping hot cups. It was lovely to have my standard morning drink of hot tea, but I knew that drinking it was probably not wise before a long day's drive. Still, I couldn't help myself. It was delicious, it was comforting, and it was paid for! But I paid for it again later, once we were underway.

We left our low-level parking lot next to Mont Saint-Michel and met the unbroken line of traffic heading *to* the island. The causeway was already bumper-to-bumper, and the little road along the coastline wasn't much better. We turned left onto the road that ran through the mainland village, then retraced our steps back toward the expressway, but took instead a smaller road leading us toward the Loire Valley. I had purposely chosen this route off the expressway for the first portion of our drive, expecting it to be more picturesque and less busy. It would also allow us to avoid some toll roads (which, at the time of route planning, was for the purpose of saving money). Of course, we didn't realize heading into our visit that driving would be a challenge, simply because the road markings were not what we were used to, and, frankly, often not very good. The countryside was pretty, but it was hard to appreciate it when we were stressed out from constantly scanning the roads and the signs, making sure we didn't lose our route.

The parts of the drive where I thought we would be by-passing towns and cities—taking a nice smooth loop around congestion—instead turned out to be painful. Often our route edged along the outer suburbs or beyond, as expected, but instead of intersections with minor roads and streets, where our highway would have had the right-of-way and we could have cruised through, we were confronted with a roundabout every mile or so. That *sounds* fine, but it meant slowing down, swooping around, and making sure we snagged the correct exit before moving on, time after time. While I had developed a fondness for the roundabouts when we couldn't make up our minds which way to drive, they were driving me crazy on this stretch, where it seemed we had to slingshot from one circle to the next, the automobile version of a monkey swinging from one tree branch to another. It took forever to make any progress.

And worse, the road we were driving on, though only a step or two down in importance from the expressway and following much the same path, did not have any bathrooms along it. I wish I had known that before I downed my additional dose of tea, because I soon started to suffer. There was no bathroom in sight, and my wimpy little bladder was stretching farther and farther. I started to sweat from the discomfort, desperately scanning the road ahead for any sign of a rest stop. Of a gas station. Of anything that might offer a bathroom.

But the roadside remained clear far off into the distance. As bladder pressure continued to build, a new discomfort (and threat) appeared: I started feeling ominous twistings in my gut, the kind of twisting I get with a stomach virus. *Oh, God*, I thought, *not Montezuma's revenge.* That didn't happen to me! I was a *good* traveler. And we would be driving half the day. The implications were dire.

"Micki, I have to pull over."

Not that there was a shoulder to speak of along the road, but I was able to pull off to the side and turn my hazards on for the short stop. Luckily, there wasn't much traffic. All the sane people were driving on the expressway. I explained that I had a pack of anti-diarrheal medicine in my backpack in the trunk—which I had NEVER had to use before—but that I was going to take now as a precaution. (I pack for all contingencies.) I checked out the dosage. I thought of the hours of driving ahead of us, of the scarcity of bathrooms. And I took the maximum amount. I don't know whether I would have had any problems otherwise, but I was safe from troubles on one front, at least.

Now, the morning tea, on the other hand, was increasing its demand for release.

There was still no bathroom on the little backwater stretch we were driving. When on the point of bursting—I was ready to pull over to a field and run behind a hedge—we changed to a somewhat larger road that soon had a rest area coming up. My foot pressed steadily on the accelerator pedal until, *oh, thank God!*, the rest stop came into view. I practically ran up to the building, which was open to the elements on the corner and allowed views into the two rooms. On the right we could see urinals (no people), so I darted left. The doors were open on the stalls in the left room, but I could see immediately that they were just showers. I figured that a unisex bathroom was on the right, a shower room on the left, and

I dashed back to the first room and entered the stall next to the urinals.

Comprehension hit. Looking down, I realized that the "showers" I had seen before were actually Turkish toilets— porcelain holes in the floor with raised platforms for foot placement—because that's what I was also looking at here. I didn't care. I was desperate. I would have hoisted my skirt and peed before a line of men, if I had had to. So I went. And went. I set some sort of personal record and felt limp with relief when I was finished.

Then I traded places with Micki, who had been holding our bags. I warned her that it was a Turkish toilet and she would want me to hold all her stuff, because there was no place to put it. So she used the toilet, too. As we were both washing up in the common sink between the two rooms, a woman came out of the room on our left. A woman who had apparently

Our Turkish toilet

been in there the whole time we were there. There was no denying it now. I had used and *then told Micki to use* the toilet in the men's room. Fortunately, there were no men around while we were there, not that they would have cared. (We were in France, after all.) Also, while not my toilet of choice, it did have a flushing mechanism and kept the area washed off and the cubicle clean. I would have been grateful for an outhouse by that point of our drive. The Turkish toilet—even a men's one—was a definite step up from that.

The *really* bad part of the day, though, was yet to come: the road tolls. We'd done tolls before, and they weren't difficult, so we weren't expecting a problem with these. But these tolls were different. We had to get a ticket when we entered the toll zone. Driving was great, but eventually we had to pay, and that's where we ran into problems. At the toll plaza, there were no signs showing any toll booths with workers—people we could give our money to—just lines for prepaid toll cards and credit cards. No little outline of an official in a hat. Unsure where to go, we got in a credit card line and hoped for the best.

It was not to be. At the front of the line, I dutifully stuck my toll road ticket into the machine and tried to pay with VISA (despite the X-ed out VISA card at the bottom of the display). The machine just spit my card back out. I tried again, and it spit it out again. Then I tried Micki's MasterCard, even though the "Maestro" card with the MasterCard logo was the *other* kind of credit card that was X-ed out in a picture on the side of the payment machine.

The machine spit Micki's card out, along with my toll ticket. The wind immediately grabbed our paper ticket and playfully dropped it to the ground ahead of our car. I tried to open my door to retrieve it, but the car was so close to the payment machine (so I could reach it through the window) that I couldn't open my door more than a couple of inches.

Micki sat next to me with both our bags on her lap so she could rummage through them for money or credit cards. Panicking that the wind was going to snatch our paper ticket farther away, I asked her whether she could get out and get it. She quickly handed me my bag and her bag and gamely ran out to hunt down the ticket.

"Libby?? Where *is* it??"

I pointed down just over the little concrete wall lining the driving lane. Micki spotted our ticket and tracked it down before the wind picked it up again. She grabbed it tight and returned to the car.

About this time, the guy who was trapped in the lane behind us started honking his horn. I glanced at him in the rear view mirror. Nearing retirement age, it looked like, he was not happy to be waiting for us. My tension ratcheted even higher, and I looked again at the payment machine for a solution. There was a red button on the machine labeled *Aider* (Help). I pushed it and produced a completely garbled cry for help in French, saying (more or less) that my American credit cards weren't accepted. The lady talked back in French through the speaker on the machine. (I asked whether she spoke English, but she didn't.) She figured out we were able to pay in cash and said, *"Un Moment,"* just a moment.

The man behind us gave another frustrated blast on his horn, his face red and grimacing in my mirror. After a moment, the Help lady spoke again, somehow disembodied behind us, but we couldn't tell from where the voice came or what she said. The entire mass of drivers waiting to go through the toll lanes could probably hear her, as she no doubt warned everyone about the idiot Americans in lane three. Maybe she told people to stop honking, which would have been fine with me. I felt stressed and guilty enough about the situation as it was, without the horns making everything worse.

Soon we saw a thin young man come from the office on

the far right side of the toll stop. He dodged the gates and traffic and eventually came over to my window. I said that our credit cards didn't work. He had me put my VISA card in the machine—only to have it rejected again—before he believed me. He opened a drawer in the end of the payment machine and slid out a keyboard, pushed a couple of buttons, and swiped my card there. Nothing happened. He swiped it again. Again, nothing.

"Card no good," he said, handing it back to me. I asked whether we could pay cash.

"Yes." He took Micki's two five-euro notes. We'd have been perfectly happy to leave it at that and get on with our trip (before the man trapped behind us had a fatal coronary). But, no, the toll man crossed back over the three lanes to the office at the side and disappeared.

Micki spoke. "Uh, Libby? Where's my credit card?"

Credit card? I drew a complete blank. It had come back out of the machine when our ticket had, but all our attention had been focused on the ticket blowing away. The card wasn't in either of my hands—I checked them both—or on my lap. I'd lost Micki's MasterCard? We both panicked a bit, looking around on the floor and in the well by the gear shift where Micki kept our change.

"Here it is!" She'd spied it on the dashboard.

One disaster averted for the day. The poor man trapped behind us seemed to give up. He still looked disgusted, but was resigned for a long wait now, draping his arms over the steering wheel. At least he had stopped honking at us.

We saw the toll guy reappear, crossing lane one of traffic, lane two, and then lane three to get to us, bringing us our change of 20 cents. He pushed something on the payment machine, the barrier gate before us rose up, and we shot through without looking back, even though an alarm was blaring the whole time. We made our escape and drove fast enough that we hoped the man behind us wouldn't pass us anytime soon, but he did, of course. I avoided any eye contact, but I could feel his glare singeing me on the way by.

Relieved to be free—and to no longer hold up an entire line of drivers—we were also shaken up by the experience and apprehensive. We soon had to go through *another* toll ticket booth to start *another* stretch of toll road, and I did it with great trepidation. *What if it happened again??* We exited the expressway before we had to pay that one, and there was little traffic in the minor toll payment plaza at our exit, so I was able to pull off to the side and investigate before driving up to a gate. I saw a guy sitting in a booth about three gates from the left, not taking tolls, just overseeing things. I carefully walked over to his tinted windows, trying to look as nonthreatening as possible in my below-knee skirt. I tapped on the glass and, when he opened the window, asked him whether we could pay with cash and showed him my coins in the amount we needed. He told me to go to the first gate—farthest right.

I went back to the car, we drove to the first gate (noticing that it was the *only* one with a green down-arrow above it), and, lo and behold, it accepted coins for payment! It was glorious! Happy day! I felt as if I'd discovered penicillin.

We continued our drive and soon found the little village of Chenonceaux. The château there is one of the most popular tourist sites in France. We stopped by the tourist information office in town, which was not very helpful, and then found our hotel. Despite all our troubles getting there, it was only mid-afternoon. We knew we couldn't check in until after four, though, so we kept driving, looking for château signs, planning to visit there before moving into our hotel. The village is tiny. The château, on the other hand, is a really big deal, so I thought we should see some evidence of it. No luck, though—we didn't see anything helpful.

That was a big difference from tourist sights in the U.S.

At home, signs and billboards in town and on all the highways announce the local attractions and direct you to them. ("Thrilling Spook Cave! Turn right in two miles onto Spook Cave Road.") In France, you wouldn't know many of the sights are *right there*, behind a neighboring stand of trees, perhaps, unless you practically stumbled over them.

As we drove on along the main street, we soon exited the little village and saw signs for the town of Cheverny (which we wouldn't visit until the next day). Now we were heading *away* from where we wanted to be. I turned around (always a trick on the narrow streets), and we quickly went back through town. This time, just outside of town in the other direction, we saw the modest sign and the drive for Chenonceau, the château. (*With* an x for the town; *without* an x for the château. Don't ask me why.) We drove onto the grounds, parked easily, used the bathroom (pleased to find actual toilets), and prepared to tour the building and grounds. I'm afraid that the lack of sleep, the stress of the drive, and not being checked into our hotel would keep me from enjoying it quite as much as I should have, but we were there, and by God we were going to see it, castle of a king's mistress, castle of a queen. We had endured a grueling day to reach this château. It had better be good.

16
Châteaux Overload

The Loire River Valley is littered with châteaux—glorious manors ranging from old defensive fortresses to elegant Renaissance pleasure palaces. Often one type evolved into the other over the years. The Château de Chenonceau, which we visited after our toll payment debacle, has an even more interesting history than other châteaux of the region. It was at one time a royal palace of King Henri II, but he gave it to his long-time mistress, Diane de Poitiers. Diane was not content with the elegant, turreted palace built in the river on the foundations of an old mill. She added an arched bridge that extended 197 feet over the River Cher to the bank on the other side. After the untimely death of Henri II from a jousting accident, his widow, one Catherine de Medici (yes, one of *those* Medicis, the Italian banking and political dynasty), evicted the mistress. She made Diane give up Chenonceau and take instead the nearby Château de Chaumont, overlooking the Loire River (and which we would visit the next day). Now in charge of the Château de Chenonceau, Catherine further modified the palace by enclosing the bridge and creating a multi-story, Italian-style gallery, so the castle itself spanned almost the entire river.

There are two formal gardens at Chenonceau, one in the style of the mistress, and—separated by a courtyard, so they don't fight, I suppose—one in the style of the widow. I know that marriage was a different institution back then, particularly for royalty, but I still have a hard time wrapping my head around the blatant and often serial infidelity that was not only tolerated at the time, but expected. I just hope that that rascal Henry was a charming fellow and his women were attracted to him for something other than his political power. Human frailty I can understand better than rank cynicism. However, there were few ways, if any, for a woman to advance herself other than through a man, so maybe I should cut the professional mistresses some slack.

Micki and I parked at Chenonceau, being careful to hide all our luggage, since the lot was not secure. We paid our entrance fee at the gate and strolled down the lane through the woods, covered by an arch of towering plane trees, a whole long, tall row of them, not at all like the sprawling plane tree we had admired in Bayeux. The cool canopy of leaves opened into a courtyard of blindingly white gravel that led to the château. We toured the building with the pack of other tourists, too many for my comfort. I heard a lot of Italian and French and a little British English, but again, practically no other American English, just a mother/daughter couple. We were most struck not by the ornate public rooms of the palace, but by the basement kitchen with all its gleaming copper pots, bowls, urns, and pitchers. Micki is exceedingly fond of copper and would have happily stowed away a kettle or two for the trip home. Fortunately for the château owners (and probably for Micki), her cross-body vault bag was far too small to hide anything larger than an old spoon. Not to imply that she helped herself to any antique silverware. Or anything else. Honestly.

Château de Chenonceau, stretching over the River Cher

After viewing the palace and taking a turn through the gardens, we ventured through the woods and found the estate's labyrinth, a formal maze constructed of shoulder-high shrubs (built by Catherine—the widow—after she claimed the property). I thought it would be fun to go through the labyrinth, but frankly, it was a little creepy in its late afternoon isolation in the woods. We didn't linger, but drove back to the hotel and started the hunt for nearby parking.

There in the center of the village, stone buildings butted right up to the sidewalks and narrow streets. Everything was tight and close and not car-friendly. Eventually we found a parking lot up a one-way lane on the backside of the long irregular "block" where our hotel was. We checked in, and I was immensely relieved that everything was in order. This was one of those places where I couldn't reserve directly on a booking page online. I had had to email back and forth with a worker, which always made me nervous that, somehow, our reservation would have evaporated before we were safely checked in. The hotel receptionist informed us that the lot next to the tourist information office would be a better location for us to park, so we moved our car. I don't know whether it was a safer location, but it was certainly closer.

When we reentered the hotel, the receptionist asked us whether we wanted reservations for dinner. We didn't know. Fine, but let them know by six. We took a menu up to our room, looked it over, and decided to make a reservation for seven. When we came down at seven, we found that the reservation had been entered for 7:30, but, hey, since we didn't speak French, we could hardly fault the lady for the mix-up.

To kill time, we walked around town. We asked the lady at the tourist information office whether there was a supermarket, because we hadn't seen one on our drives through the village. We missed the convenience of our Paris supermarket, where we could pop in to get bottled water or fresh fruit. But no, she replied, there was nothing in town but a bakery. We were less than a half-kilometer from the third-most-visited château in France (after Versailles and Chambord), and there was nothing in the village except two hotels, two or three restaurants (one closed for the evening), a pottery shop, the bakery, and a gourmet fine-foods shop, where we could have bought *foie gras* and probably canned snails, but not the basics we were looking for. We would have been much happier with apples, bread, cheese, and chocolate, the staples of my life as a traveler. The village was so tiny that we quickly ran out of things to look at and had to return to our room to finish filling the extra half hour until our reservation time. I started writing my notes for the day.

Supper, when we got to it, was delicious. We both ordered the tomato-mozzarella-green salad (the Sicilian, I think it was called) and a ham-and-cheese crêpe (mercifully without any raw egg yolk). I had two *boules* of ice cream for dessert (*parfum aux choix*—I guess *parfum* means flavor as well as scent— and went with raspberry and lemon). Micki had *crème brûlée* again. She was well on her way to developing an addiction, it seemed, and who could blame her? We both had wine to drink. The meal came to nineteen euros for me, so at least under $30, this time.

Having already exhausted the entertainments of the town, we retired to our room for the rest of the evening. It was a smallish, oddly-shaped space with some walls that did not meet at right angles. Our bathroom "shower" was a detachable hose in the bathtub that was tucked under the eaves, cramped by the ceiling, so it really had to be a sitting shower. Other than a few errant sprays across the walls and floor, we managed just fine.

I was enjoying Micki very much as a travel companion— she's just about ideally suited for my style of touring: follow an itinerary planned in excruciating detail but be open to change, if desired. Still, I missed my family terribly in the lonely quiet of rural France. This was the day my son Paul (Not French. Trust me.) had a commercial shoot for being a winner in a TV station's "What I Want to be When I Grow Up" essay contest. I was able to get the report on the phone that night, because we weren't limited by mysterious implosions here. Paul was very excited. In addition to the commercial shoot, he had received a whole backpack of prizes, including four passes to Adventureland theme park outside Des Moines. With my easy motion sickness, the rides at a theme park held no attraction for me, but my little blues guitarist was happy, and his older sister was thrilled.

This was the second consecutive night that our hotel TV had no English channels. Related, perhaps, to the lack of English we had encountered on Mont Saint-Michel and at the Château de Chenonceau? I felt keenly my inability to speak French properly and wished I could find a nice German speaker somewhere, so I could actually communicate and not feel like such a foreign-language laggard. On Mont Saint-Michel the previous evening (had it really been just one day earlier??), we had watched an Elvis special, where at least his singing was in English. In Chenonceaux, we were reduced to watching a funniest videos show—stupid, but at least it made sense in any language. I was reminded of the time my grandmother and I had been stranded in our airport hotel with our delayed flight. We thought that a TV with nothing but French stations was lonelier than no TV at all.

Since we were having a quiet evening around our hotel room, I finally got around to trimming my bangs with the only tool I had on hand that could remotely tackle the job: my tiny manicure scissors. My shaggy bangs had been driving me crazy for a couple of days. Earlier that morning, when we were trying to kill time before embarking on our long drive (trying to lessen the tea left in my bladder before the big trip—not that *that* worked so well), I was going to use the time to whack off some of the length that was hanging in my eyes. But that wasn't possible, because we had already hauled our suitcases to the car, and all my sharp things were in my suitcase (rather than in my carry-on bags) because of flight restrictions. My goodness, our efficiency was sometimes too great to deal with.

That evening, though, bored in Chenonceaux, I remembered, and I very inexpertly nibbled away on my bangs with a set of tiny, 5/8-inch-long curved blades. It wasn't a great cut, but I did get the worst of the excess length removed. (My hairstylists hate this tendency I have to go rogue with my bangs. *I* hate paying the price of a trim just to get my bangs cut, and then usually shorter than I like and in a shape I don't. The hairstylists are following haircutting rules, I know, but my face and hair just don't cooperate. We compromise by me not getting my hair cut professionally very often.) I captured the short hair bits in a towel and then shook them down into the box of purple petunias outside our window.

When dusk was falling (the sun seemed to set very late while we were there), we all of a sudden heard some raucous meowing, followed by wolf whistles, and any number of odd sounds. Our room overlooked the restaurant patio, and we looked outside for a bird—the sounds seemed as if they were coming from the hedge of trees on the left. Eventually, Micki located a big bird cage on the patio below us, which, we later discovered, contained two parrots. Their noise was intriguing and interesting for about five minutes. After that, they became incredibly annoying. They did, at least, shut up before we went to bed at full dark. Once we were back home and I finally looked at the various brochures I had collected on the trip, I saw that the hotel pamphlet featured a parrot named Charlie. It didn't list who Charlie's friend was.

The next day was lovely. Not only was the weather again perfect, but we had no toll roads between our destinations. We had breakfast at the hotel restaurant, and it was quite good: croissant, baguette, butter, jams, honey, drink, OJ, grapefruit juice, boiled eggs, yogurt (flavored, too!), two kinds of cereal, milk (bad), fresh fruit salad, and pound cake. We loaded up for a long day.

It didn't take long to haul our suitcases to our little car, and then we were off. We got diesel at the edge of town, but I forgot to use a credit card to get a receipt (so I hope the IRS doesn't audit me for this business trip). But, you see, I wanted to break a 50-euro note and the 38-euro fee was a good amount for that. There was a lady attendant who came out to fill for me. I don't think that in all my years of driving and filling up on fuel, I had ever had a service attendant before. It felt very strange to be waited on. I'm sure we paid for the service, but I didn't care, as long as we got the fuel we needed. Let a professional worry about diesel versus unleaded for once. We got a half tank, but I don't know how many liters that was or the cost per liter. Exorbitant, I'm sure. Welcome to Europe, where they pay about twice the price for fuel that Americans do because of higher taxes and fewer government subsidies. And good for them, I say, because their roads are generally excellent and their cars much more fuel efficient.

We drove without any major problem to the next château on our visit list, Chaumont. That's not to say we didn't have our moments. We had some trouble finding our road along the Loire River and drove back and forth on the very same stretch of blacktop looking for it, probably five or six times, because I *knew* it must be there somewhere. Oh, those French road signs.... In the end, we took the turnoff that looked on the map like it *had* to be it, even though we couldn't find a road number to confirm it. And it was, indeed, the road we had been looking for. *When* would we adjust to that playful French tendency not to label the roads in a way we could identify?

Chaumont is a lovely white château with fat towers, looming above the Loire River on a site that was originally defensive. It was owned (among many others) by Catherine de Medici, queen of France, and she entertained astrologers there, including the famous Nostradamus. This was the château that Catherine gave to Diane, Henri II's mistress, when she kicked Diane out of the Château de Chenonceau. I'm sure the trade must have been a step down for Diane, but it was hard to feel too sorry for someone who ended up with this fairy-tale wonderland. Even the trees on the grounds were magical, giant spreading cedars of Lebanon, with their spooky, reaching branches. They looked like they had come out of Harry Potter's world. I was enchanted by it all. The stone gatehouse leading into the castle was once the home of guard dogs, as well guard humans, and a large stone doghouse was built into the wall right next to the guard house.

The fairy-tale-like Château de Chaumont, on a bluff over the Loire

Embraced by three castle wings, an open courtyard looked from the bluff down to the river.

The whole complex was delightful—large enough to be impressive, but small enough to seem actually livable. Although I don't think either Catherine or Diane had anything to do with this, there was also a dog cemetery in the woods, where a pet elephant (an *elephant!*), Miss Pundji, was also buried. The large, luxurious stables—also added much later—even included a special kitchen for the horses. I imagined that the indulged horses on the estate probably lived better than the average peasant of the age.

One reason we visited Chaumont was to see the world-renowned, internationally acclaimed Festival of the Gardens held there every summer. The château was great, but the gardens were not at all what we expected. They required a separate ticket to enter, and we followed a broad path that led to the displays. That part of the property was divvied up into separate blocks, where different gardeners or floral designers—who had submitted designs for the chance to exhibit—expressed their artistic visions along the theme of the year, which was "Body and Soul" when we were there. Paths led from one stylized garden to another, and next to the entrance to each bay, there was a sign explaining what the design was attempting, an extensive philosophical treatise on each one.

There were 25 set pieces, but we left after viewing about one-third of them. They were so bizarre, so strained and artificial that we couldn't even enjoy them. They were the floral and horticultural equivalent of the "artwork" we had seen in the Pompidou Museum. My favorite of the ones we viewed (and realize I'm using that term in its mocking sense) was about returning to the womb. Visitors followed a path hedged-in by curved willows that spiraled around to open into a small central round area (the womb). There we could sit in wicker lounge chairs, if we wanted to relive the experience in utero. We were stunned by the intent of the display. *Why?*, we wondered. Micki and I clearly lack the artistic sensibility, the intellectual heft, to make the giant leap to abstract art. Just give us a pretty garden. That's really all we ask.

Off we drove to the next château on our schedule: Cheverny. We would have cut this visit out if we'd gotten interested in the gardens and stayed late there, but I'm so glad we didn't. Built by a count, whose descendants include the present owner, the château for a while belonged to King Henri II. He gave it to—get this!—Diane de Poitiers, the mistress we've already met, but she preferred Château de Chenonceau and sold this one off. One wonders whether she preferred Château de Chaumont to this one, as that's the place she ended up with. Still, she made money off the deal, so she must have known what she was doing.

The noble family still lives on the third floor of this château. We had a chance to be mild voyeurs when we toured

A family relaxes in the "womb" at the Festival of the Gardens

the interior of the palace. Family pictures stood on a table in one of the halls, and a very handsome family they were. One of the highlights of the visit was seeing all the hunting dogs—dozens of them, anywhere from seventy to more than a hundred, according to various sources. Even the dogs were handsome—lean black, tan, and white—although they were taking their siesta while we were there, so we didn't exactly get to see them in action.

Had we managed to be there at their 5 p.m. feeding time, however, *that* would have been a sight to behold. The pack barrels down stairs to their concrete-floored kennel, baying and wriggling with excitement. Their handler keeps them away from a line of raw meat pieces and what looks like dry food by swinging a whip back and forth between them and the vittles. (I've seen a tourist's video.) When the dogs are all ready, the handler gives a command, steps back, and the dogs descend on the food, snapping up the meat and carrying it off to eat in (relative) peace. The dogs are active hunting animals, and when the pack races through the hunting grounds, that sight has to be impressive—and terrifying to any prey they pursue.

The château is still fully decorated with period furniture, unlike the other châteaux we had seen, which were stripped almost entirely bare. The creamy white building is in a classical style, very clean, very symmetrical, with rounded domes and bell towers. I didn't like that there were no trees near the palace—the August sun was glaringly bright on the surrounding gravel—but otherwise, the château and the grounds were lovely.

We drove on, then, to Château de Chambord with no

Hunting dogs rest at Château de Cheverny

difficulties, just more stress than we really should have experienced. (We're gifted that way.) The drive to Chambord ended, as several of the château drives did, with a long, straight shot through a dark hunting forest, down a narrow lane lined on both sides by tall trees with peely bark—lime trees, I've read, but not the citrus kind. (Maybe European linden trees??) These were royal hunting grounds, and even today they are loaded with game. We passed road signs warning us of deer (no surprise) but also signs warning of wild boar (a new warning, for us).

At Chambord we entered our first pay parking lot in the Loire Valley. The parking area was huge, row after row spread over three large lots. We took our little parking ticket at an entrance gate, found a spot, and then walked to find our hotel, as we didn't see any other way to get into the village proper. As we walked toward the cluster of buildings that composed the little village, through the closer parking lots—all full— we were awed by the magnificent structure we could glimpse through trees and buildings, towers topped by innumerable

Château de Cheverny, still in the family of the count who built it

prickly chimneys. Our hotel was easy to find in the tiny village; it was a converted hunting lodge right next door to the giant château, directly across a lane from the gardens.

We asked the desk clerk where we were supposed to park, explaining where we currently were. He told us to quickly go back and move our car during the "no-charge" window (the first half hour?), drive past the lot for the tour buses, turn left to the gate with the special intercom button, and push the button to buzz him.

We did that, and the gate lifted to let us drive right up to the hotel and park next to it. There we were, in the middle of the royal grounds, in a controlled lot. Why was it that we got so stressed out about driving? We always ended up— eventually—exactly where we wanted to be. We didn't have accidents or even altercations. So far, we had been honked at once in a roundabout on our first day of driving, and then by the impatient man stuck behind us at the toll payment machine. That was it. You'd think we'd at least driven to the wrong end of the country or something—unexpectedly finding

Château de Chambord, originally a hunting lodge for King Francois I

ourselves in the Pyrenees—the way we got so anxious about taking to the road.

We hauled our bags to our room and found it to be plain but spacious. There was a separate toilet room and a room with the sink, shower, and bidet, all in a muted yellow with white painted trim. This hunting lodge apparently kept things simple, which was fine with us. We went outside to visit the château before it closed for the day.

The Château de Chambord is enormous, 440 rooms, with 365 fireplaces and 70- or 80-some staircases. (The count varies, for some reason.) It is the largest château in the Loire Valley, and the second-most visited in the country after the Palace of Versailles. There were hundreds of tourists there at the time, maybe even thousands (supposedly the château receives up to 8,000 tourists a day in the summer), but the building and grounds were so large that nothing was crowded. We wandered around and marveled at the size and grandeur of the building. I enjoyed locating some of the many copies of salamanders

Salamander emblem of Francois I

that adorn the palace—perhaps an unexpected design detail, but the salamander was King Francois I's emblem, and the palace contains more than 700 of them, according to one of my guidebooks.

Construction on the place started in 1519 by 25-year-old Francois, to be used as a hunting lodge. Its building required the draining of a swamp and the diverting of a river to achieve his plans—but complete construction lasted longer than Francois I did. The king died in 1547. His son Henri II (we've crossed paths with him several times in the last day) took over construction for a while, but the castle wasn't completely finished until 1685, during the reign of Louis XIV.

It was fun to wander around on the extensive roof, where ladies of the court would observe their menfolk shooting game on the grounds. The roofline is famous and celebrated because of its many chimneys, and the double-helix stairway is also well known, designed, perhaps, by Leonardo da Vinci himself. We took a quick turn through the carriage museum in the former stables. It included some royal coaches that had been built for the man who thought he was the legitimate king for much of the 19th century—Henri Compte de Chambord—but he never managed to ascend to the throne, however sound his royal lineage was, and the elaborate coaches were never used.

By this time, the sun was sinking in the sky. We were at our third château since getting up that morning and were a little tired from being tourists, so we didn't explore the grounds as much as we might have otherwise. We certainly didn't rent a rowboat and pull ourselves along the Grand Canal to the Cosson River, as we could have. Rather, we crossed the quiet road and returned to our hotel, where we would eat supper. When we entered the restaurant, the hostess asked whether we wanted to sit *interior* or *exterior*. OK, we could handle that kind of French. Definitely outside, on such a beautiful evening.

The waitress handed us our menus and disappeared. We looked at the listings in stunned silence. The menu was entirely in French, and not the kind that showed up in my phrasebook dictionary, so it was basically undecipherable for us. We either looked perplexed enough, or the waitress saw us looking into a dictionary, because she asked whether we would like an English version of the menu. Would we?! Bring it on! Most of the food was game-based, which wasn't normal food vocabulary. And even the translated versions left some room for guesswork. We both ended up choosing a stew-like dish made with venison or *biche* (doe). I can't remember the term they used for the little hush puppies or croquettes, but I asked about them ("potato?") to make sure they weren't going to make the venison meal a bad choice by getting us, say, an accompaniment of breaded kidney of wild boar. Knowing that French cooks like to use all parts of the animal, I was cautious.

After we ordered, another English-speaking group took the large table next to us. They looked like three generations of a family. As they struggled with the same French menu we had, we clued them in about the English version, which they were very grateful for. With the ice broken, we both started talking about our trips. They were renting a villa in the Loire Valley, as they did every summer, and had recently driven from La Rochelle, on the Atlantic Coast. I was enormously gratified to hear that they, too, had been having trouble with the road tolls. These visitors had smart chips in their credit cards, and *still* the cards usually didn't work in the toll booths. The father of the family said he'd been pushing the help button when they ran into trouble, and they'd had cars piling up behind them, too. Kindred spirits! I just hope that the irritated French drivers who had to wait for them at these toll payment traffic jams realized that those were *Canadians* holding up the show, not more clueless visitors from the United States!

The meal was delicious. For the starter, I went with the cantaloupe half with port wine in the hollowed-out middle, and Micki chose the salmon mousse with sour cream. She thought my choice was revolting, and I thought her raw salmon was disgusting. (Oh, puh-leez. Who has ever heard of disliking cantaloupe but thinking raw fish is just fine?) I fully expected Micki to get sick for the last part of our trip, but she seemed to suffer no ill effects.

Our venison stew and potato puffs were both excellent, and we rounded the meal out with a lemon dessert. I do like those French set menus. We probably wouldn't have ordered dessert anywhere, à la carte, but, hey, if it was part of the set menu, we'd be glad to take it! When the waitress wanted to know whether we were finished with each course, she would ask us, *Terminé? Fini?* And we were. We're not good at dawdling, not even during our meals. The French may be able to stretch a meal out to a couple of hours, but that's not the Lutheran way. The Lutheran way would be to eat quickly, leap up and clear our own table, then gather the dishes that the neighboring diners were done with and take those straight to the kitchen, too. And then grab a pot of weak coffee (decaf, at that hour) and go around the whole dining room topping off cups. Clearly, the French were not Lutheran.

The next day was to be our last in France, and we wanted to be up early to get on the road, so we retired to our room for the rest of the night. Micki took her shower first and cried out shortly after shutting herself in that room,

"Libby! Can you come in here?"

I found her wrapped modestly in a large white towel, looking frustrated.

"How the heck do we turn this shower on?"

It was a new one for me, too. The controls had two knobs, one on the left and one on the right, but they weren't for hot and cold water. After a little testing, we discovered that the

Château de Chambord, with 440 rooms and 365 fireplaces.
We stayed off to this side in a converted hunting lodge.

one on the left controlled water pressure, and the one on the right was for the temperature. That was the limit of our experimenting with the equipment. We never tried the bidet, although I should have turned it on just to see what the spray was like. Our own little fountain.

Unfortunately, we were not able to call home this night. Our room phone did not dial out with a "0," and if we wanted to use it, we would have had to pay by the implosion. It looked like the fee was anywhere from one euro a minute to a euro for four minutes, depending on which rate would apply to us. For a trans-Atlantic call, we would surely pay the highest rate. We hadn't seen a public phone either, so we would just skip this night and call the next, trying to use up our remaining 7,000 minutes. (*Could* that be possible?? When we used the France Telecom public phone, we only had about 70 minutes left.) In any case, we expected to be able to call from our airport hotel, and we would talk, talk, and talk endlessly, as we are both fully capable of doing.

The grand château outside our hotel had a fancy laser light show after darkness fell. We were so tired, though, and it didn't get dark until so late, that we didn't go to it. Plus, the official light show cost a fistful of euros, which also persuaded me to give it a miss. Still, we could have checked it out from outside the official viewing area, helped ourselves to a cheat peek. When would we ever again see the massive, magical palace illuminated in the dark?

But Micki was asleep, and my hair was all wet from my shower, and we willingly gave up our chance. Too bad. I'm sure we missed a glorious sight. Or a really cheesy tourist rip-off. It's sometimes hard to tell the difference.

17
More Than a Candy Bar

Our final day in France took us through some of the most celebrated, historically interesting châteaux, right in the heart of Three Musketeer country. It also took us closer to Paris, the airport, and all that city traffic, but we would be comfortably outside the vehicular chaos for most of the day. The tradeoff, of course, was ill-marked, narrow country roads, but I think we preferred those to the pressure of roaring trucks and impatient *autoroute* drivers.

We started the day with another tasty breakfast at Chambord, perhaps the best we'd seen. Everything was on the buffet table except our drink, so we could help ourselves to as much as we wanted. With fresh, warm, crusty white rolls tempting us from a basket, we helped ourselves to quite a bit. As for the hot beverage, it was good that we *couldn't* help ourselves to as much as we wanted. (Some of us are slow learners when it comes to sensible fluid intake.)

As usual, I had a lovely pot of tea, and Micki had a pot of *chocolat*. I should note that the hot chocolate was not the thick sludge I had tried to drink in Italy years earlier, but a creamy, more normal hot chocolate that Micki said was very good.

We left Chambord a bit reluctantly, because we knew we had to go through another ticket toll to get to the next château on our itinerary—Fontainebleau—and then eventually we'd have to brave the traffic around Paris and the airport. My stomach got an early start on its little dance of anxiety.

But the trip to Fontainebleau was successful, even the toll ticket part. There was not much traffic on the expressway at that hour, and when we came to the pay section of the toll, I told Micki we were just going to go for it. I picked a line with a green arrow—at the right end, since our cash payments had all been on the right end so far. We held our breath. If we had troubles, I was just going to have to push the "Help" button again. But no! We drove up in the green-arrow lane, and the ticket machine took our ticket and our money! No spitting either back out! We had coins at the ready, but we could even have used bills. Eureka! Had we finally figured out how to use the toll ticket payment machines, on our very last time through one??

In the town of Fontainebleau, we drove down a narrow little street and suddenly saw a Parking sign for the château, although we had seen no sign of the château itself. So we ducked into the underground parking garage and hoped for the best. The garage had a grippy gray rubber floor that the car wheels squeaked on. We had to drive down two levels to find parking, and every time I turned the wheels we heard them squeal on the rubber floor. It sounded like a basketball court in the middle of an intense game. But the building was clean and well-lit. We just hoped it was close to the château itself, since we had no idea how far away the palace still was. After carefully locking up our luggage, we walked up the two flights of stairs to street level, and, happily, there was the estate wall right across the street, with a fancy gilt-edged iron gate just half a block away.

We ended up entering the property from a side court, passing extensive buildings that used to house the stables, it looked like. But we had no trouble finding our way to the château, where we received recorded tour information with our ticket. The palace was so large and rambling, we weren't always able to match up the room we were viewing with the correct recording, but it was a pretty impressive place, all the same. This château, like Chambord, had also been started by Francois I in the 1500s. It, too, was added to and changed over the next 300 years. Napoleon, in particular, aimed to embellish it so that it would rival the palace at Versailles—which he did not care for—in lavishness and beauty. The Palace of Fontainebleau now houses more than 1,500 rooms, compared to the (mere) 700 in the Palace of Versailles.

We started out by touring Napoleon's private apartments, which supposedly contained a lock of his hair, but we never saw it. What we did see was Napoleon's copper travel toilet and silver travel bidet, for the best in bathroom hygiene when away on military campaigns. His mobile bidet resembled a fumigator pump, an elongated cylindrical piston with a long curved nozzle. It looked like it should be used for spraying rose bushes. But, of course, that was not what it took aim at. The items were simply and discreetly labeled and displayed, leaving their use to the viewer's imagination, but still, a toilet and bidet?? What a way to humanize the great general and emperor!

This was another royal château that was incredibly grand, elaborate, and luxurious. Perhaps its most famous feature is the horseshoe-shaped staircase leading up to the main door, where Napoleon descended and abdicated before his exile to the tiny island of Elba. (The exile didn't take. Ten months later he escaped and returned to the mainland, where he led troops for another 100 days until his defeat at Waterloo.)

After a whirlwind visit (it was disgraceful how quickly we

08/18/2010

The famous horseshoe staircase at Fontainebleau

flew through these glorious cultural sites), we remembered to
pay for our parking at the garage *before* returning to the car,
which was a small miracle, really. Where we come from, parking ramps are few and far between, and the ones I do use on
occasion (a couple of hours away from home) do not require
paying before departure. We left the parking ramp through
a different exit than we had entered, and we didn't know at
first where we were or what direction we were heading. Fortunately, we quickly realized we were driving back down the
same street we had come into town on—back in the direction
of Chambord—which would take us right back to where we
had started the day. I turned down a street or two that got us
going roughly in the direction we needed to.

But, of course, nothing about driving in France was really
that simple for us, so we had to guess and bumble our way
to the next large town, where we were able to follow signs
to the city of Melun that would lead us by our next château,

Vaux-le-Vicomte. Melun was the first time we saw an American-style freeway, where it was built through existing neighborhoods by elevating over them and relying on exits in a city rather than roundabouts. We successfully followed the expressway through and around the city and grabbed the exit we needed on the northeast side. From then on, we were on small country roads until we came to the sign directing us to the château, down a long, straight lane of those tall, straight trees. We were able to park in a free lot right across the road from the palace complex.

The château itself wasn't exactly overwhelming—we'd seen much more impressive. Not that the place wasn't beautiful and impressive—it was—just not as much so as the ones that came after it (or before it, on our itinerary). What made it so terribly interesting was its history. The ambitious young Nicolas Fouquet, superintendant of finances for Louis XIV, planned an elaborate estate, employed a trio of the best architect, landscape architect, and painter to design it, and bought and demolished three villages to achieve his vision. He spent vast sums of money on the project and reputedly employed 18,000 workers. As the first of the great châteaux, its grandeur and beauty outshone any royal palace of the Sun King and enraged Louis XIV, who had his financier Fouquet arrested. The new palace was simply too sumptuous, too luxurious, to have been funded by legitimate means—or so Louis was convinced, at any rate. Charges of misappropriated funds may well have been trumped up by a jealous political rival—Jean-Baptiste Colbert—who aspired to take Fouquet's position in the government.

To show who wore the biggest wig, Louis subsequently built the palace at Versailles in an attempt to eclipse the size and refined beauty of Vaux-le-Vicomte. Then he confiscated all the furnishings of the château and took them off to Versailles for himself. Louis wanted Fouquet put to death, but he didn't succeed in that. The poor man was simply imprisoned for nineteen years until his death in 1680. The whole story and intrigue form the basis of *The Three Musketeers* and *The Man in the Iron Mask* series, which I really wanted to read after viewing the château and grounds.

Later, after we returned home, I did download the entire series (for free!) on my digital reader. What swashbuckling adventure! What fun and romance! What devious doings and evil intrigue! Today's soap operas have nothing on the historical grounding and imaginative embellishments of author Alexander Dumas. I loved reading the scenes in the story set at Vaux-le-Vicomte and Fontainebleau because *I had just been there!* I could *see* the young lady-in-waiting hiding in the woods and declaring her love for King Louis. They walked the very paths that I had!

I have only two complaints about the series, and since my copy cost me nothing for boatloads of entertainment, my

Vaux-le-Vicomte, the château that enraged King Louis XIV with its grandeur and elegance

criticisms don't amount to much: 1) The length of the series is daunting, three to seven volumes, depending on how they are divided up. My own version consists of *The Three Musketeers, Twenty Years After, The Vicomte de Bragelonne, Ten Years Later, Louise de la Valliere,* and *The Man in the Iron Mask.* It's exhausting to work through the whole story. A real commitment. Some marriages last less time than it takes to read the entire D'Artagnan series. And, 2) the series has a terribly sad ending. It was awful. I bawled my eyes out. My advice to anyone taking on the books is to stop before reading *The Man in the Iron Mask.* Sure, you think you have an idea of the story, with some dashing image of Richard Chamberlain as Philippe, rightful heir to the throne in France (or Richard Chamberlain as Philippe's identical twin, Louis XIV). Foolishly, you think the last book is just going to focus on *that* story. But, no. The other characters are there, too, with a terrible, terrible ending. Trust me, you really don't want to experience it.

But awareness of the story did heighten my enjoyment of the château at Vaux-le-Vicomte. After touring the main rooms of the palace, we climbed through the attic—redolent with the musty smell of bat droppings, although none could be seen—and up the spiral staircase to the dome, where we could look out in all directions and appreciate the layout of the celebrated gardens and the various stables and courtyards. Then we went down, and then down some more, through the basement, where we could see the kitchen and a barred cell, where a wax figure wearing an iron mask sat on a straw bale. This château was interesting in that it had wax historical and literary figures in period dress in several different locations, such as attending a ball upstairs, working in the kitchen downstairs, and other places where they dramatized scenes from the Three Musketeers story.

I know some people find wax figures hopelessly hokey, but I thought they helped bring history to life, and I appreciated

Wax figures of Nicolas Fouquet and his wife

Three Musketeers wax figures

seeing some of the dress and hair fashions of the time. The men had long flowing hair, capes, and broad-brimmed hats adorned with plumes. (Fouquet himself was quite dashing and handsome, if his wax figure and a carved bust of him can be relied on.) The women were either weighted down with luxurious heavy gowns (upstairs) or wearing plain work clothes (downstairs) in the kitchen. The rich women had cascading ringlets of hair; the servants' hair was straight and covered by bonnets. I'm not sure what it says about contemporary society, but the poor workers looked a lot more "normal" than the high-society versions did. I guess practicality and comfort have won out over ostentation and extreme fashion.

Next we walked through the acclaimed formal French garden designed by André le Nôtre (the biggest landscape architect of the day, who later designed the gardens at Versailles), but we didn't go all the way across the canal to the far reaches. (I, for one, was too conscious of what we still had to accomplish for the day and didn't want to put it off too long. The later in the day we left, the heavier the traffic would be.) Finally, we went through the carriage museum, where we saw numerous coaches, carriages, and carts, many of them again peopled with wax figures.

We wandered back outside. Apparently, there was an old-person's outing at Vaux-le-Vicomte for the afternoon, which was hard to fathom, given the physical demands of touring the property, but we saw it. Some of the elderly could barely get around on the pea gravel. The wheelchairs were having a hard time of it. One old woman was slumped over on a bench outside the bathroom. A French woman asked whether she needed help, but she already had help coming, was what I got out of their exchange. Strange. Micki and I took one final swing through the bathroom, complete with two stalls that contained Turkish toilets. (People avoided those, so it wasn't just us finicky Americans).

We left Vaux-le-Vicomte and began our guesswork toward
Roissy and the airport. We quickly decided just to take the car
directly back to the airport rather than try to find the hotel in
Roissy and then drive to the airport. For one reason, it would
be much easier to follow signs to the airport than to try to
figure out how to get to Roissy and *then* to our hotel. Neither
of us was up to extra city driving with no useful directions.
Eventually, we found our way to the appropriate expressway,
which was a little confusing, because we had to exit it briefly
for another numbered expressway, then rejoin our original
road. But we managed.

Once we saw listings for the airport, I no longer worried
what anything was called or where it took us. I just followed
the signs with the plane on them. Traffic was much heavier
here than anything else we'd seen (not counting the bumper-
to-bumper back-up heading through the tolls in Normandy),
with lots of trucks, so I really had to pay attention. As we
got nearer to the airport, we saw signs for a BP gas station
next to the highway, so I zipped in there and we filled up to
return the car. I paid in cash but requested a *reçu* (receipt) for
my records. The clerk didn't know what I was talking about.
A helpful man waiting behind me said, *"un ticket"* ("tee-kay").
I repeated, could I have a *ticket*, please? Oh! A *ticket*! Certainly!
And he gave me a receipt for my cash sale.

We reentered the traffic throng and kept following signs
to the airport until we were in the midst of airport exits and
signs with no idea where to go. I missed the first Information
stop we saw, but caught the next one early enough to pull off,
park on the side, and walk to the big information board. I
had guessed (remembered?) earlier that we would go to Terminal 2, and eventually I found the car rental information
on the big map and confirmed that, yes, it *was* Terminal 2. So
we were golden from there, just looking for the Terminal 2
signs. We also started seeing the car-key sign for car rentals,

so we were really happy now. Would it, could it, possibly end that easily?

Once we got onto the oval road in the center of the terminal, we were home free, because we knew from our previous round and round attempts to figure out how to get *out* of the airport exactly where we needed to go to get back *in*. Yes, it was all familiar. We did one lap around so we were in place to exit downhill to the car parking area, took the sharp left into the half that included Avis (first experienced in our shuttle van), turned left about halfway across, drove to the back of the lot, turned by the little Avis house, and parked in the express check-in spot. A man was at our side before we could even remove our junk from the car. He asked for the keys, checked the mileage, saw we had no damage, and gave me a receipt for exactly what the charge should have been, all before we had our bags out of the back.

From there we trundled into the terminal. We found an information desk upstairs, where we planned to ask the man working there about where to find a shuttle for our hotel. But first we had to wait quite a while for the young American man in front of us to line up his hotel for the night. He wanted one in Roissy that wasn't too expensive and would be on the train line to head into Paris the next day. He quickly learned that there *were* no hotels on the train line, and the best he could do was to take the shuttle to his hotel, and then ride the shuttle back the next day to take the train to Paris.

When it was our turn, we asked about the shuttle to the Mercure Hotel in Roissy. The airport worker wasn't sure whether the shuttle had changed its pick-up point for the summer, as many others had, so he called the hotel and confirmed that, yes, that was the case. He instructed us to go to the end of the terminal where the trains are. So we lugged our suitcases and trudged with our other baggage to the far end of the terminal, which was chaos, filled with people waiting for trains, rushing to catch trains, or getting off trains.

We tracked down another information desk upstairs, where the worker did not speak so very much English (although more than I could French, probably). She told me we needed to go behind #5. I figured she was talking about the lines, so we headed down the escalator to the tracks, and saw that behind #5 was nothing but train track. There was no way that was where we were supposed to catch the hotel shuttle, unless we could pull off some Harry Potter magic and enter a different realm to get there.

We rode up the escalator and returned to the help desk, this time getting a different worker who was much more helpful. She told me to take the elevator to the 5th level and wait *there*. So we crammed into the elevator with everyone else and their luggage, and as the elevator halted on other floors (we started on 2), other people crammed in with *their* luggage, until we could hardly move. The Italian family on the elevator found this all very amusing. I liked them better than whatever nationality was all put out about having to share. Sure, they had been the first ones on, at the train level, but they were hogging all the space with their loaded luggage cart.

At level 5, we stood outside at a bus stop. We eventually figured out (OK, I asked two women pulled over in a white van that looked shuttle-ish, and they *told* us) that each shuttle had listed on the side and the front and on the scrolling display above their windshield *which* hotels that particular bus served. Somehow, I had missed this observation on my own. If we had been heading to Holiday Inn, we could have had a couple of possibilities before *our* shuttle finally arrived. But arrive it eventually did, and not that many people got on, so we were able to sit for the ride to Roissy.

The ride seemed to take forever, with loop after loop to get there (We gave not-so-silent thanks that we weren't driving.), but probably only took 15-20 minutes. The bus stopped at a couple of other hotels before ours, then pulled up right to the door of the Mercure. We went into the large, open, mostly empty lobby. The hotel is a four-star establishment and seemed very comfortably "American" after the funky places we had been staying. We were helped at the check-in desk almost immediately; again, we were placed on the second floor (first floor, in France). We paid in advance.

Micki and I took our cases to our room. She flipped a light switch. Nothing happened. She tried a lamp. Again, nothing.

"Why don't the lights work?" she wondered. Were all the bulbs burned out??

I had fallen into this no-electricity trap before, in Italy, and I looked around for a slot to put our key card into so we could activate the electricity in the room. But nothing looked like any card slot I had seen before. So we tried the lights individually, to no avail. I was about ready to call the desk when I looked around the entry area again and realized that the lighted square way high next to my head *wasn't* a nightlight, but probably the key slot. I slipped the key card right in and *voilà!* Suddenly we had light.

We rode the elevator downstairs to the hotel bar/café for supper. We had almost identical meals: the chicken club sandwich with tzatziki, tomatoes and French fries, followed by a brownie with ice cream. I had mineral water. Micki had wine. It was wonderful. The food was good. The prices were very reasonable compared with what we had been paying. And it felt incredibly good to know we were rid of our car and all its stresses and responsibilities. *And* to know we were returning to our families the next day.

We checked on Internet access (expensive!!) and telephone options before returning to our room, as well as when the shuttle would run the next morning. We were advised to use the telephone booths next to the lobby rather than call from our room, which would be expensive (more implosions, no doubt). Micki was not able to get hold of Jeff, so she left a message for him and turned the booth over to me. I was able to reach John, but had forgotten that early Wednesday afternoon in Iowa, they would be heading to drum lessons and were, in fact, in the car then. So I talked with Emily a bit and told John I would call back during Emily's lesson. I went back to the room to kill half an hour. We were enjoying the five (*five?!*) English-language stations on our TV, in our BIG room, with its BIG bathroom. Well, big shower/sink room. Again, the toilet had its own room.

With the English-language TV accompanying us sweetly in the background, we worked on repacking for our return flight, which was a pleasure, because *we had enough room to do it!* After cramped and odd and bare little rooms across France, we had American-like space to spread our possessions out, American-like, as was our national expectation, if not an actual birthright. Micki took her shower and discovered that our modern hotel shower again had the dual control knobs that our old converted hunting lodge had. I decided I'd better mention that configuration in my French traveler's book rather than ignore it, as I'd planned to. (In the end, however, because of space limitations, I ignored it after all. Hopefully, my language and culture readers will find the tip in *this* book!) When Micki was done, it was time for me to go back downstairs for a phone call, and since I had more than an hour's credit on the Telecom phone line, I planned to talk a lot. Which I did, but even I couldn't drain all the units left on the phone card. My family just wasn't that talkative on the other end. Then I went up to take my shower and get ready for bed.

It was our last night in France. We had been on a wonderful adventure, but we were ready to go home.

18
The Way Home

Micki and I wanted to make sure we didn't oversleep. Our flight was for 10:45 in the morning. That sounded comfortable enough, but we planned to follow the American guideline of getting to the airport four hours early for an international flight, so we wanted to make sure we were there by 6:30 to check in. We didn't know for sure how long we'd have to wait for a shuttle, so we set my alarm for 5 a.m. As a backup, we also set the alarm on the TV. The programming instructions said not to turn the TV off when using it as an alarm, but to leave it in standby mode. Unfortunately, nothing explained what standby mode was or how to get it, so we ended up muting the TV, but leaving it on. That seemed like a reasonable precaution, but it really disturbed my sleep, with all the images flickering through the night. I think I was in bed by ten, and Micki was even earlier.

My alarm beeped dutifully at 5:00. I shut it off, and we both dragged ourselves up, even though we were still tired. I turned the TV off, as we'd no longer need that alarm as a backup. At 5:10, the TV started beeping. So I *could* have turned it off and gotten some decent sleep? In the long run, it didn't matter. Yes, we were short on sleep. We were certainly not at our best mentally or physically. But we were ready to start the trip home, and we were both happy about that.

Micki and I were quickly ready for the day, checked out, and waited about ten minutes for our shuttle. We were the first ones on it. In fact, we were the *only* ones on it. For the whole ride.

"You realize," I told Micki, "we're probably going to get to the airport before it's even open." It had happened to me before, in Italy.

Well, the airport was open at 5:50—when we arrived—but there was no one working the Delta/Air France desks. We snagged seats where we had a good view of the line of empty counters, settled ourselves in for the wait, yawned yet again, and then Micki went to buy us croissants.

Eventually, a security guard showed up, wandered around a bit and gave us hope that other workers would appear, but no, he went over to the security section and sat there. Later a number of women arrived in Air France uniforms and disappeared behind the counters, but we didn't see any more of them. Then the security guy ambled back and sat at the last desk in the Air France section. I went and asked him when check-in would open.

"Oh, about 7:30, or so."

Finally—*after* 7:30, I will note—some official-looking people came out and sat at the first couple of Air France check-in desks (on the far left end of the bank of counters, while we were sitting at the far right. Of course.). By now, other people had started to mill about, and by the time we got down to the correct end of the section, there was a line of travelers stopped at the opening to the expansive cattle chute that would lead us to check-in. A man with loads of luggage was blocking the way and keeping anyone from entering. Well, we had had a long wait already and were tired of that, so I ducked under the ropes of the zigzagging chute—row after row—and headed straight up to ask the man at the counter where we should be. (Micki was sure I was going to get shot by one of the alert military guards with their submachine guns.) The man directed me back to the line because the workers weren't ready yet.

Back in line, we waited impatiently until finally the check-in clerks were ready. An elegantly polished woman quizzed us before allowing us into the zigzagging rows to wait there: Where we were going? The young American in front of us was flying to London, and the lady told her to go down to C-something to check in there. *Sheesh*, I thought, mentally rolling my eyes. *She didn't even know where her check-in gate was?* Then, at our turn, we told the elegant lady that our destination was Minneapolis-St. Paul, and she sent us way the heck over to the C terminal, too. *Why, why, why* can't planes stick with their assigned locations?? Especially when we get there so early to wait for them!

It was a long haul to Terminal C, and once there, we again faced lines, but not too long, at least. The lady working in *this* section confirmed that the line we were in was for Minneapolis-St. Paul and somewhere else—Cleveland, I think. Just those two flights. We got through the passport check quickly, checked in quickly, and got our boarding passes. As we hurried to our gate, Micki noticed that there was a small store right before security and asked whether I wanted to get John his Prince Roll cookies, since they were a favorite of his and I hadn't had a chance to get to a grocery store since Paris.

I popped into the store, got the Prince Rolls and two packs of chocolate-covered butter cookies (my own favorites). We went through passport control and then security with no problems and didn't even have to take our shoes off! It was a long walk to our flight gate, but there were plenty of available seats in the waiting area when we got there, so we camped out and got as comfortable as we could. I went to get us drinks, a couple of Coke Lights from a machine. Slowly, the area began to gather more people, including a man with a baby in a stroller, but the rows of chairs never filled up. Before long, the crew announced priority boarding (there went the baby), and then boarding for our section.

We got in line behind one young African man and before another. The one in front of us had on a green sweater and a red-and-white striped knit scarf around his neck. And he had absolutely killer, burn-your-nostrils-out body odor. It was so bad that we tried to give him plenty of room ahead of us, but the smell still just about knocked us over. When we had been in Paris, we had occasionally encountered someone in the métro or in a museum who could use a good deodorant, but nothing like this guy.

Micki and I looked at each other in unison, eyebrows up, registering that the stink here went off the smell-o-meter. The man behind us was somewhat better (and it helped that he was behind, rather than ahead). *He* had on a red-and-white striped Oxford shirt and jeans. He was very thin and very nice and had tried to entertain a little girl who was with her daddy, while we were waiting to board. The guy in front of us reached a gate control person before we did, of course, and I swear the airport worker backed away from him. There was some question about his paperwork, though, so the man ahead of us got held up, and Micki and I got to board the plane before he did. We were greatly relieved and hoped we would be seated in entirely different sections.

We were among the first in our particular part of the plane and had an entire storage section above our heads to pack our bags into. Eventually, others followed, and our storage bin filled up, but it was nice not to have to battle to get our carry-ons in.

We had no sooner settled into our seats than Micki said, "Oh, no."

Green Sweater Guy was heading down our aisle, and he stopped two rows ahead of us, sitting in the end seat, right across the aisle. When he lifted his arms up to place his luggage in the bin above, the blast about sickened us, as far back as we were. We felt sorry for the people who were sitting closer to him than we were. And the *other* B.O. guy had a seat in the middle section right behind him! Then, when a family wanted to sit together, he kindly switched places with one of them and ended up in the middle section *right across the aisle* from me! Fortunately, the thin guy tried to sleep for most of the trip and wrapped himself up with a blanket from head to toe, sometimes sitting up and sometimes lying on his side, but either way cutting off the odor.

Green Sweater Guy continued to emanate, however. I went to the back of our section to ask the flight attendants whether there was a chance of being able to change seats, but they said it was a full flight and we probably wouldn't be able to. Coming back, I was hit by the smell starting two rows behind my seat, which was four rows behind Green Sweater Guy. And every time he readjusted, it blasted out stronger than ever. I'm sure he was an intelligent, considerate person who had simply been raised in a different culture than us hyper-hygienic Americans. I'm sure he had a wonderful personality. Who knew how long he had already been traveling, how long since he'd been able to shower? He seemed to be an adventurous spirit, crossing several continents on his own. He was nice looking and neatly dressed and completely positive in myriad ways. But there was no avoiding the sorry fact that he reeked. I don't know how the people around him were able to survive the flight, let alone eat.

The two or three rows directly in front of us were filled by U.S. college boys, possibly on some sports team. While college boys wouldn't normally be my first choice of flight neighbors, we were glad to see them, because we knew they would be freshly showered and deodorized. And they were, not only fine smelling, but also nice, well-behaved young men. They could have been the Brigham Young chess team returning to Utah, as far as we could tell. No complaints about them, whatsoever. Eventually, Green Sweater Guy got chilly and put his light blue windbreaker on, which was a godsend, because it didn't breathe. Thus, the remainder of the trip was more bearable for the rest of us.

The flight was not memorable, otherwise. It left on time. It flew on schedule. There were no screaming babies. I finished my small pack of chocolate-covered butter cookies. (Micki helped, but not much.) We did notice that the return flight, with its American crew, was much colder than our flight over had been, with the French crew, which had been pretty warm the whole way.

As we approached Minneapolis-St. Paul, a flight attendant announced that we would need to pick up our luggage and take it through customs. After claiming our checked luggage, people who were leaving the airport were supposed to follow the red line to the left, and people who were transferring to another flight were supposed to follow the *gray* line to the left. We soon landed and got off the plane and entered immediately into a passport control line, which was moving fairly quickly. As Micki and I neared the front of our line, we saw that other groups traveling together, such as a mother and son in the next line, were going up to the control officer together, so that's what we did when our turn came. We figured that if either of us was going to have any sort of trouble, we wanted to be there to support each other.

The very nice customs officer told us we should have come up separately, but went through his list of questions anyway. No farm visits. No agricultural products. Had we bought anything in the airport? I said I'd bought some packaged cookies in the Paris airport. He said that was no problem. How did we know each other?

"Friends," Micki said, at the same time I said, "Through church."

Were we on a mission trip? We laughed. "Oh, no! No mission trip." We were so happy to be on American soil and able to understand everything around us that we were in ridiculously good moods. Then the guy repeated that we really should not have come up together, that he didn't want to get sued.

"We wouldn't sue you!" I said. "We're so happy to hear English again!"

He explained that if either of our passports had brought up a felony report on his computer, and he'd had to ask us about that, then he could be sued for revealing that information to the other person, who may not have known about it. Ohhhh. OK, so we won't do that again.

After passport control, we had a very short walk to get to the baggage carousel, which was already conveying suitcases around. Micki's suitcase (purple with a pink belt) came out fairly soon, but I was fooled by a couple of red suitcases before mine appeared. I was sure that was it on the far side of the carousel, though, and I grew somewhat alarmed when the nice African guy (red/white shirt) pulled it off and looked ready to walk off with it. I started hustling around the crowd along the length of the carousel to cut him off before he went through customs with the wrong bag (*my* bag). But he looked it over some more and realized that it wasn't his and put it back on the conveyer belt. Relieved, I returned to Micki, and when my suitcase came around, I hauled it off.

Now we knew we had to look for a gray line to the left. We headed left out of that hall, and as we approached the exit into the terminal, we saw a red line and a gray line in the carpet leading off to the left. We followed the gray one, which put us in line to go through customs. A young man came up after us and asked whether this was where we were supposed to be, and we said that the airline had told us to follow the gray line if we were connecting to another flight. He must have been doing that, too, because he stayed behind us. The people in front of us were going through custom checks, opening their bags. We had nothing we were worried about, though, so we waited patiently for our turn. We noticed that at the far right counter, Green Sweater Guy had been pulled over and was having his bags searched. (We didn't envy anyone *that* job!) The customs guy pulled out a huge blue plastic bag that looked like it was full of ears of corn. He dumped them out of the bag, and we saw that they were bananas. A big bag of bananas, directly from Africa? Or do they grow bananas somewhere in Europe?

Before we could see what happened to him and his contraband, a harried, gray-haired official in a white shirt, dark pants and displaying some sort of badge came rushing up to us and asked us where we were going. He looked at our boarding passes and gestured to the exit at the right.

"You're supposed to be over there. Over there! You should all be over there!"

He was flushed with anger—as if we'd intentionally irritated him—and his wispy gray hair flew about. We wandered toward the exit, but I went back to explain that the airline had told us to follow the gray line to the left. He cut me off.

"Get over there!! Don't you people *listen?!*"

Red-faced and carrying too much weight, he looked like he was going to have a heart attack. So we went over to the exit, where—what do you know?—there was *another* set of gray and red lines. We soon went through the customs check there—it was pretty much just a matter of walking past a worker at a lectern. On the other side of the exit, a very nice volunteer asked where we were going and directed us on how to get there. We let her help us, even though we didn't need it, just because she was so pleasant and well-meaning. We were still in shock from the unaccountable rudeness of the customs official who had yelled at all of us. It would have taken him no more time or effort to be courteous and tell us we didn't need to be in the line for declaring items. What a jerk. Unfortunately, he gave a very bad impression of U.S. airport officials.

We hauled our bags and hiked waaaaaay to the end of Terminal C for our next flight. Eventually, an overdue flight at our assigned gate resulted in our flight being moved down a couple of spots. We didn't care. Everything was going swimmingly. We had both called home on our cell phones to assure our loved ones that all was fine and we would see them soon. Micki got herself a magazine and a book. (She had finished hers on the main flight. I still had a good bit of *Jane Eyre* to get through, though.) I bought a coffee, figuring that, since we'd been up since ten o'clock the previous night in local time, I could use a little caffeine boost to get me through the rest of the day.

Our final flight boarded on time and left on schedule. It was, again, on a small plane and space was very tight, but we were able to cram our carry-ons aboard. We were seated near the back of the plane, and there were older people sitting behind us, very jolly older people. A white-haired woman told us that this was the party section of the plane, and everyone behind us whooped and giggled. We couldn't help laughing with them. While the older set may have had a party flight, I was glad the flight was short and I had a good book to distract myself with, because we soon hit a long patch of strong turbulence. I found myself thinking, as our plane dove and pitched, that, *Sure—we'd made it all this way just to die in a plane crash when we were almost home again.* But things evened out and we ended our flight smoothly.

As always, it seemed that we had to wait forever on the plane before we could leave it, but then we had just a short walk down toward the main waiting area, and there was Micki's Jeff, ready to take us home. We had to wait a little longer before our checked luggage appeared, but soon everything was there. We were trying to tell Jeff about our trip ("Don't you people *listen*?!"), and he was telling Micki about what had happened locally while we were gone.

The drive home passed quickly. Jeff had brought a cooler with cold Diet Pepsi in it, which Micki had repeatedly requested from France. I declined to take one, though, between not wanting any more caffeine and not wanting to have to stop on the way home. We pulled up in front of my house earlier than expected. I hauled my suitcase out of the back, hugged Micki and thanked Jeff, and happily carried my bags inside to reunite with my family.

German
Shepherd

Elizabeth Bingham

An Excerpt from

German Shepherd:

A Guided Tour Through Germany and Austria with a Faithful Companion

It was Jeff's own fault that his wife left him for Europe again.

The four of us were sitting together at a Valentine's dinner—Jeff and Micki, John and I—and I showed Micki a magazine I'd brought along that featured a renowned garden festival we had visited in France four years earlier. A completely weird garden festival that we had ditched after viewing only a third of the displays (and this after *paying* for it, mind you, that's how bad it was). The year we had been there, the theme was "Body and Soul." Maybe the theme showcased in the magazine, "The Seven Deadly Sins," would be better, but I wouldn't hold my breath.

French artistic flights of fancy just did not appeal to our hearty Midwestern practicality. We came from Germanic stock. Micki's heritage was almost all German. Mine was British with some German thrown in. We lived in an area of the country heavily settled by Germans. Our wide feet were planted solidly on the ground, and we were not into Frenchified intellectual whimsy.

Jeff generously (foolishly?) told us, "Hey, you girls should go to Europe again! You could go in August, after I get back from my business trip."

My mind started humming. August might well work for me this year, because my family's annual vacation to the north had been moved forward a month. After vacation, before the start of school. . . .

Poor Jeff never knew what hit him.

The day after he threw out that suggestion, I consulted with Micki to see what our combined travel windows were, and by the next day I'd mapped out a possible Alsace/Mosel/ Rhine trip, combining the wine countries of eastern France and western Germany.

We talked about it during lunch with another friend, and I said that anyplace was possible that time of the year. Our friend Treasa was pulling hard for Ireland, but when I mentioned, "Or, we could go on a *Sound of Music* tour," Micki audibly sucked her breath in, unconsciously indicating where she would really like to go.

By that afternoon, I had laid out a Berlin/Bavaria/*Sound of Music* tour. We would start in Berlin so I could see my adopted German mother again after a seven-year lapse, then head down to the land of beer and *Brezeln* (big ol' pretzels), Mozart and mountains.

I ran the prospect by my husband, John, already feeling guilty about such a selfish pleasure, but happy that he supported me going.

I asked Micki whether she was OK traveling two weeks this time instead of the twelve days we had used for our trip to France.

"I think it will be fine," she assured me.

"Are you sure?" I persisted. "Because I could take a day off Berlin and a day off Austria and get it down to twelve days."

"No, no. Two weeks will be fine."

"But what about Jeff? Will he be OK with that?" Jeff adores his high-school-sweetheart wife and relies on her heavily to help run their farm, business, family, and home.

"I'll talk to him about it later, but I'm sure he'll be fine with it."

So I continued planning for a two-week trip. I called Inge, my German "mom" in Berlin. She was delighted to hear from her "Libbymaus," using the "mouse" suffix that she adds as her favorite endearment. She wrote our projected visit on her calendar. And what was the name of my friend? I told her my good friend was named Micki and assured Inge that she was very nice. "Mickimaus!" was her immediate response.

Oh, boy, I thought. *Micki's going to love that.*

By the next day, I had reserved lodging and a rental car and for several weeks kept an eye on the non-refundable airfare offers. Ticket prices remained stubbornly high. Finally, airfares dropped a bit, and I thought we should probably go ahead and lock in our flights. I checked in with Micki, we chose the flights we wanted, and I bought our tickets.

The trip was on—we were going to visit Germany and Austria.

A couple of weeks later, she told me that she and Jeff had been talking about their summer schedules, and he asked her when we would be abroad. She gave him the dates, Aug. 6-19. He noted them on his calendar.

"But that's two weeks!"

Apparently, she'd told him that we might be gone a little longer than before, but had neglected to say when exactly that would be. He immediately started suffering separation anxiety. Micki assured him he would be fine.

Every day I tried to hit the treadmill now, adding slowly to the length of my walk, because I wanted to be in better shape if I was going to climb every mountain. Frankly, though, it was an inconsistent effort, and there were not enough months between February and August to get myself truly fit. Not with the effort I was willing to put into it anyway. I hoped that Micki had also slowed down some the last couple of years.

In May Inge called from Germany to greet my husband on his birthday. We were out, so she left a message wishing him well and expressing how much she was looking forward to seeing Libbymaus and her friend Mickimaus in August. I made sure to tell this to Micki, of course, who groaned and feared she would be Micky Mouse the whole time we were in Berlin.

In June Inge called again for my daughter Emily's birthday. She didn't mention Mickimaus this time, but warned me that it was terribly hot in Berlin, around 100 degrees Fahrenheit all week. German homes don't have air conditioning or even fans, for that matter. Micki's plan for beating the heat took a liquid bent. "I guess we'll have to drink a lot of beer to stay cool."

In mid-July I was on my way to meet Micki and another friend for lunch. This social occasion would also serve as a German-trip-planning meeting, because Micki and I had both been too busy to discuss our upcoming travels, and other than the basics of when, where, and how we were traveling, we didn't know what was going on. That would not do for a couple of control freaks who needed to know—in detail—what the plan was.

During lunch, Micki and I discussed what we would take, basically the same as for our French trip—a 21-inch suitcase, a backpack, and a tote bag each.

"I could never pack for two weeks in a suitcase that small," our friend, Jodi, said.

"You'd be traveling, Jodi!" I said. "It's OK to wear things more than once. Fresh socks and underwear, but other than that, it doesn't matter."

She looked skeptical.

"I'm learning!" Micki piped up. "I really can get by with less."

Jodi was unconvinced. I tried again. "As long as it's not visibly dirty or smelly, it's fine to wear again. You'll be around completely different people from day to day, so they won't know you're re-wearing something. And Germans wouldn't care, anyway. They're not hung up on clothes."

Jodi still disapproved. I didn't give up.

"When I worked in an Austrian school, it was not unusual for teachers to wear the same clothes for a couple days in a row. In fact, there was one teacher who wore beautiful, stylish, expensive outfits. She'd start the week with a gorgeous fresh outfit and then wear it every day of the week."

"Oh, my God. . . ." Jodi looked like she was going to vomit.

What a difference between Americans and the Europeans I know! Honestly, it's been so long since I was an English assistant in that Austrian school that I no longer remember whether that woman wore her outfits for a week at a time *every* week, but it doesn't matter. What matters is that no one else in the school seemed to care or even notice it. The clothes were clean. She looked fabulous. Why on earth waste the money and energy and water or dry cleaning to wash after one wearing, when that just causes the clothes to wear out that much more quickly?

I thought of the summer I stayed with Inge outside Berlin in 1994, less than five years after German reunification, when she and others in the former Eastern sector were still lagging behind the West in material standards. She washed her laundry in the bathtub, wringing it out by hand, and after rinsing in the same tub, hung everything out to dry, either in the backyard or the basement. I washed my own clothes next to her at the tub, because I did not want to add to her burden.

After my short stint as washerwoman, my back ached and my wrists and arms throbbed from the forceful wringing of wet clothing.

In 2000 when I visited her again, she had a small portable machine that "cooked" the clothes in hot water, which eased the process, and then in 2007, she had a small washing machine in her basement, a sight almost as welcome to me as it must have been to her. Anyone who thinks nothing of tossing every top or pair of jeans into the laundry after one tidy wearing should try doing their laundry by hand, just once. I predict that they would very quickly decide that no harm would come from giving those clothes a second wearing, or a third or even more.

Today most German families have access to a washing machine, but washing laundry still takes valuable water and expensive energy, and it's still fine to re-wear clothes. I planned to do so.

Our departure date quickly approached. At the airport going through security, I had to slip off my shoes, of course, my trusty hiking sandals that had seen me through untold miles of walking in France and beyond. This was a brand-new pair, though, one I'd worn just long enough to make sure I wouldn't blister from them. I was starting the trip with fresh footwear.

Micki, too, had a brand-new pair of the same sandals. We didn't know we were each updating our favorites, but it wasn't surprising. She had worn hers to our local fair to break them in and somehow, nowhere near the animal barns, had stepped in cow poop the very first time she'd worn them. They have good, deep hiking treads. After one wearing, she had to power wash her new shoes. I couldn't help laughing when she told me this, finding it far more amusing than I should have. I trust she got them well cleaned, as they were currently in her suitcase.

Our first plane, from Cedar Rapids to Chicago, was an aged American Eagle model, but at O'Hare we switched to a spanking new Berlin Air A330 Airbus. It was gorgeous. Everything was shiny and spotless. We all had individual viewing screens, like iPads, set into the seatback in front of us, but with no after-market wiring boxes blocking our foot space as we had suffered from on previous flights. In the night, I even managed to doze off despite the flight noise—until a mighty snore woke me. I realized with horror that *I* had produced the guttural roar. I glanced around self-consciously and hoped no one had heard me.

We were sandwiched between a selfish young American woman in front of us (who fully reclined *two* seats for the trip, to most fully inconvenience Micki *and* me) and a couple behind us whose nationality we couldn't determine, but who couldn't move, get in, or get out of their seats without grabbing, pulling, kicking, or pushing our seat backs. Our seats became their personal leverage stations anytime they moved around, which was a lot. It was not a restful flight, and we were relieved to approach Berlin.

I was surprised that, when our German plane landed, the largely German crowd did not clap. In the past, flights with lots of German passengers usually burst into applause after a safe landing. Although I had always found the practice hokey and silly, I kind of missed it now.

After the usual airport confusion of claiming luggage, hunting down an ATM that would work with our American cards (surprisingly difficult), and figuring out transportation to the nearby village we wanted, we used the bathroom and then took a bus to the Berlin Zoo stop. There we entered the cavernous train station and, after a few questions, located the platform where our regional train would arrive.

We had a few minutes to wait, so I finished my bottle of water from the plane. Turning to place it in the multi bin recycling station next to us, I gestured with the empty bottle to the opening I thought was correct and looked questioningly at an older lady who was standing there.

She nodded that I had the right one, then she asked where I was from, and we got to chatting. She told me that I spoke *ausgezeichnet Deutsch* (excellent German). I thanked her, and we kept talking. After frustrating trips in France and Italy with only the most basic communication skills, it was a joy to speak a foreign language I was fluent in, in a culture I was familiar with.

We discussed her elderly parents—92 and 89 and failing now. She was on her way to place her mother in a home and was tired and stressed about the situation. Micki and I were tired and stressed from jetlag and lack of sleep. It's amazing any of us managed a coherent conversation. The woman repeated later how excellent my German was, so I told her that I had lived in Austria for a while.

"One hears that," she responded.

I was not surprised. My German is a Heinz-57 mix of influences, from many years of German teachers and Austrian teachers and extended stays in both those countries, each of which has a great deal of regional variation. (Even native German speakers can't understand all the dialects.) While hardly a pure "native" accent of any kind, my particular speech serves well to disguise my nationality and leave people guessing where I'm from. Austrians often suppose that I'm German by my accent, while Germans hear the southern pronunciation. As long as they take me for some sort of real German speaker, I count that as a language-learning victory.

If conversation gets difficult and I start making noticeable mistakes, the next nationality I'm most often identified as is Dutch, which also makes me smile to myself. *Ah*, I think in satisfaction. *They don't hear an American accent!* It took many years to overcome my American vowels and our broad, flat

American "r," so any compliments are a welcome stroke to my ego.

Our train arrived, the German woman on the platform wished us a good visit, and we entered our car. Inside, Micki and I tried to shove our luggage in tightly and make it as small as possible to take up as little room as we could, but fortunately we didn't seem to be depriving anyone of a seat. The modern train raced smoothly through its stops. We arrived in Inge's village, dragged our bags off, and trudged the short distance to her house. We were already wilting in the heat. A full hour earlier than expected—about 9 a.m.—we rang her bell. She welcomed us with hugs and smiles, as did Hans-Jürgen, her partner of many years.

"What can I get you?" she asked immediately. There is surely not a hostess anywhere who can out-welcome Inge. She is unfailingly generous and kind to visitors.

All we wanted was water, so she gave us sparkling mineral water, which tasted great. I learned years ago to like sparkling water, since that's what Europeans usually drink. I was surprised, though, that Inge had commercial bottles of the stuff, because last I knew, they carbonated their own tap water so they didn't have to lug the heavy glass bottles to and from the grocery store. With no car (I'm not sure that either could even drive), they needed to haul all their purchases on foot, and they weren't getting any younger.

I learned a little later that they had won a case of bubbly water in a contest. Here was Inge, giving the "best" to us, and we were gulping it down by the bottle, trying to overcome our dehydration from the flight. We were unintentionally chugging down their special supply, no doubt carefully hoarded to share with company. Plain water would have been fine for our purposes, and I asked to switch to the homemade bubbly once I realized what was going on.

Inge took us to our apartment on the second floor (the

"first" floor, in Germany), we cleaned up, rested a bit, and then went downstairs at noon for lunch. Our three-room apartment (with private bath) had been a rental unit for years, but now Inge kept it as guest quarters for her many visitors.

Downstairs, she provided her usual delicious and filling midday meal. She had made us goulash, boiled potatoes, and green beans with butter crumbs on top. It was wonderful, but we were so, so tired. And, as always, she wanted her guests to eat more than they wanted to. To us, it felt like five in the morning—we'd essentially been up twenty-four hours straight, and *that* after sleeping poorly before our trip—and we weren't hungry.

I had forgotten to warn Micki not to eat normally at Inge's. She needed to slow way down, to leave food on her plate, but she didn't know that. As soon as Inge saw an opening appear, she swooped in and tried to get Micki to take more food. When Micki politely declined, Inge came around the table and put more food on Micki's plate, whether she wanted it or not. I was familiar with this insistent generosity and had developed strategies for evading it, but Micki was defenseless.

Ever polite, Micki tried valiantly to eat the extra food but had to give up. I ate her last cube of meat so it wouldn't go to waste, but she did leave some food on her plate. That was a smart if unintentional gambit, because the only thing Inge hates more than people not eating "enough" food is people *wasting* food. I had used this knowledge to my advantage in the past, warning her that I could not eat any more, and if she put more food on my plate, I was not going to eat it. It's just about the only threat that can put the brakes on her loving over-solicitousness that everyone get plenty of food.

She's not trying to kill her guests with kindness, although I sometimes feel that will be the effect. As a child, she was a refugee from East Prussia (in present-day Poland) after World War II. The war and its aftermath were a harrowing experience, and those who went through it knew great hunger and even starvation. To many of those former refugees, food still means much more than required fuel. It symbolizes love and welcome, prosperity and, I suspect, survival and triumph over a harsh past.

John and I have a good friend who lives in Hamburg, Germany, and her mother was also a child refugee from East Prussia. When we stayed at her home, the mother also welcomed us with great warmth and hospitality and one evening prepared a grill fest, a real feast of meat, for our small group, including chicken and sausages, pork and beef—a heaping mound of at least five different kinds of meat, just for the four of us. We were kindly but firmly encouraged to always eat more, eat more, until we were stuffed. Wanting to be polite, we ate as much as we could bear.

When I mentioned something to our friend Heidi about *all* the meat her mother and brother had prepared, she explained that it was in our honor and was meant as a compliment. It was very sweet of them (and very costly), an overwhelming generosity that may have stemmed from Helga's childhood deprivation and current security, the same source as Inge's great urge to feed others well past any possible hunger.

At the end of our welcome meal with Inge and Hans-Jürgen outside Berlin, I saw that their paper napkins still lay neatly folded on the table, never touched. Ruefully, I looked at mine, a wadded, shredded, mangled mess next to my plate. I've noticed this tendency for years. Apparently, napkins are purely decorative for most Germans. I don't know how they keep their mouths and hands clean—it's not like they wipe their mouths with their sleeves or their hands on the tablecloth. I could never look presentable without using my napkin during a meal, and somehow I always manage to destroy it. By the time I'm done, it sits in pitiful contrast to the perfect, untouched napkins of my German friends.

It was the same with Germans of our own generation that we would eat with later. And with those of my daughter's generation. They don't touch their napkins but somehow they remain completely presentable. Even after all these years, it's a mystery to me.

As it was, Micki and I were lucky to have arrived early enough to have our delicious meal, even though we were too tired to appreciate it fully. Inge is very old-school when it comes to food, and had we arrived late in the day, it would have been open-faced sandwiches for us instead.

Years earlier I had arrived at Inge's with a friend in cold November, after we had driven hours from Dresden and then stopped at a time-consuming sight on the way. We were famished. Inge was so disappointed that we hadn't been there at midday; she had made a venison goulash for us, but when we hadn't arrived by early afternoon, they had regretfully eaten without us. She instead served us tasty brown bread with a wonderful selection of cheese and cold cuts, supplemented with attractively cut fruit and raw vegetables, everything laid out artistically. It was all fresh, healthy, and plentiful, and we were encouraged to eat our fill.

The next day my friend Lynn and I spent seeing sights and returning our rental car. We arrived back at Inge's again starving, because we hadn't eaten anything beyond a light snack. Oh, she exclaimed, it was too bad we hadn't been there for the hot meal! They had had the venison goulash again, and it was so good! Open-faced sandwiches again for supper.

The following day, again sightseeing in cold Berlin, we met a German graduate-school friend of mine for lunch, and my American friend and I had our first hot meal in the Berlin area, in a restaurant. I told Dorothee how we had missed the made-for-us venison goulash two days in a row because we weren't home for the midday meal. That we were *starving* when we'd arrive at the end of the day, because we didn't really eat when we were out and about, and we would love to have a hot meal then. Would it kill our dear German relatives to heat up the goulash in the evening instead of reserving it for midday?

My German friend laughed and said that her mother would do exactly the same thing. That was the traditional German way. The hot meal is for the middle of the day. Evening is for something lighter, almost always open-faced sandwiches. I sighed, knowing that already, but still incredulous at how unbending the social rules were. Inge would no more think of serving a hot stew in the evening than I would consider serving beer for breakfast. As it was, the last of the (no doubt delicious) venison goulash was being eaten while we were in the city that third day.

Years later, Micki and I would enjoy the benefits of a good hot meal or two with Inge, because we were with her during the day. If people really wanted to lose weight in Germany, though, I would suggest staying with an older German and skipping lunch. Those guests wouldn't starve by any means (they'd get plenty of good food), but they wouldn't need to worry about overeating. (Which, come to think of it, is a pretty good idea. We in the U.S. could learn a thing or two here.)

Micki and I were at Inge's in time for the goulash this time around, and we suffered the effects of *too much* warm food rather than too little. Sleepless and stuffed, we retreated to our rooms for a while to recover.

Stay in Touch

If you enjoyed *French Twist*, please consider reviewing it on Amazon.com or Barnes and Noble.com.

Follow Elizabeth Bingham on Facebook at www.facebook.com/pages/Elizabeth-Bingham-Author/681013812044922.

To hear about new books first, sign up on Elizabeth Bingham's New Release Mailing List at http://eepurl.com/bp3jtn. This is for new release notification only.

Index

Other Books by Elizabeth Bingham

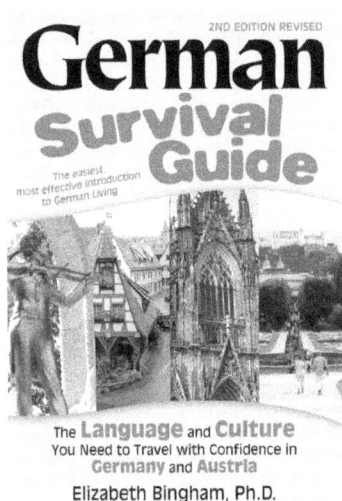

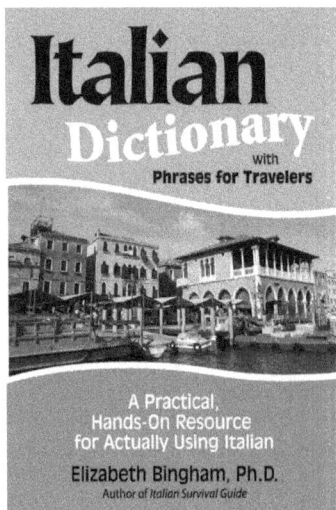

French
Survival Guide
The easiest, most effective introduction to French living!

The Language and Culture You Need to Travel with Confidence in France

Elizabeth Bingham, Ph.D.
Author of *Italian Survival Guide*

Italian
Survival Guide
Revised Edition

The easiest, **most effective** introduction to Italian living!

The Language and Culture You Need to Travel with Confidence in Italy

Elizabeth Bingham, Ph.D.
Author of *French Survival Guide*

2ND EDITION REVISED

German
Survival Guide
The easiest, most effective introduction to German Living

The **Language** and **Culture** You Need to Travel with Confidence in **Germany** and **Austria**

Elizabeth Bingham, Ph.D.

Italian
Dictionary
with **Phrases for Travelers**

A Practical, Hands-On Resource for Actually Using Italian

Elizabeth Bingham, Ph.D.
Author of *Italian Survival Guide*